MW01097069

Table of Contents

Introduction

The Massachusetts Tests for Educator Licensure (MTEL): General Curriculum Exam is designed to prepare elementary teachers for the classroom by ensuring that they have a strong knowledge base in the content areas that they will be expected to teach. These content areas are tested via two subtests—the Multi-Subject subtest and the Mathematics Subtest.

The Test at a Glance

Test	Multi-Subject Subtest	Mathematics Subtest
Format	55 multiple choice questions (90% of subtest score) and 1 open-response question (10% of subtest score)	45 multiple choice questions (90% of subtest score) and 1 open-response question (10% of subtest score)
Topics	• Language Arts (30%) • History and Social Science (30%) • Science, Technology, and Engineering (30%) • Integration of Knowledge and Understanding (10%)	• Numbers and Operations (41%) • Functions and Algebra (22%) • Geometry and Measurement (18%) • Statistics and Probability (9%) • Integration of Knowledge and Understanding (10%)
Time	4 hours total per test session + 15 minutes for a computer-based testing tutorial and non-disclosure agreements	
Method	Both subtests are computer-based. For the open-response questions on each subtest, you will be asked to hand-write and then scan your response. Calculators are not permitted on either subtest. On-screen calculators may be provided during the Mathematics subtest. You may not bring your own.	

Each of these subtests has multiple topics that will be explored in the rest of this guide.

Language Arts

Reading and language arts are foundational for student success. Students develop skills in reading, writing, and speaking that demonstrate comprehension of written and spoken texts, a command of the mechanics of the English language, and critical thinking skills.

Test Structure

The Language Arts section makes up 30% of the Multi-Subject subtest. Within Language Arts, there are five major subcategories with which you must be familiar:

A. The History and Structure of the English Language

B. Works of Literature and Literary Analysis

C. Literary Genres, Elements, and Techniques

D. Literature for Children

E. Writing and Composition

Each subcategory is divided into topics, which state the skills you must be able to demonstrate on the exam.

The History and Structure of the English Language

The English language has come to its current form over a long history of development through contact with other languages. This section covers the history of the language, as well as the structures and conventions of Standard American English today.

Topics Addressed:

1. The History of the English Language
2. Diversity in the English Language
3. Fundamental Language Structures
4. Grammar and Conventions

Historical Development

The history of the English language is generally divided into three periods—Old English, Middle English, and Modern English.

Old English (approx. 400-1100) developed as the result of the invasion of the British Isles by the Anglo-Saxons. These Germanic groups brought with them their language, which blended with that of the Celts already living in Britain to form Old English. Old English sounds very different from Modern English, but there are many modern words that have roots in this earliest form of the language.

Middle English (approx. 1100-1400s) developed following the Norman Invasion of 1066, led by William the Conqueror. The Normans brought their language, a version of French, which gradually diffused with Old English to create what we now call Middle English. People used the Latin alphabet to write out the sounds of their spoken language. The spread of English literacy and the standardization of the language was greatly aided by the invention of a printing press with moveable type by Johannes Gutenberg in 1450.

The language continued to evolve as the English were increasingly in contact with other cultures. What developed (and has continued to develop) was Modern English. The first English dictionary was published in 1604. New dictionaries are published each year, as new words are added to English vocabulary.

Borrowings and Derivatives

Languages are constantly evolving and new words are introduced. Two ways in which new words have formed in the English language are through borrowings and derivatives.

A **borrowing** is a word that has been brought into one language from another with little to no change from the original.

Examples:

- Borrowings from Greek and Latin: *drama, podium, encyclopedia*
- Borrowings from French: *leisure, prestige, poultry*

A **derivative** is a word formed from another word or words. One type of derivative involves different forms of the same word. For example, derivatives of the word *depend* include *dependence, dependent,* and *dependable.*

Derivatives can also be created by combining other words. The component words have very different meanings and when they combine to form a new word, the derivative has an entirely different meaning from the words that created it. Examples include *blackmail, butterfly,* and *jackpot.*

Diversity in the English Language

The English language is not the same everywhere. **Dialects** are specialized versions of a language, typically found among specific regional, social, or other cultural groups. Dialects are most evident in oral language.

Dialects can employ their own vocabulary and grammatical patterns that are distinct from those of Standard American English, which is the dialect of English used in academic and business settings. For many students their home dialects can have important cultural meanings for them.

Dialects should not be invalidated, but students can learn that fluency in multiple dialects (including Standard American English) can provide them with the skills to read, write, and speak appropriately for different settings.

Fundamental Language Structures

There are certain fundamental structures that make up the English language. These include phonology, morphology, syntax, and semantics.

Phonology

Phonics is the understanding the sounds and printed letters are connected. Groups of sounds (with their associated letters) are organized into sequences to form words. Phonics provides a way for students to decode and encode words based on their component sounds.

Phonics follow certain predictable patterns. Within the system of phonics, there are letters or combinations of letters that make certain sounds. Words that contain these same sounds are said to contain the same phonics pattern. Teaching phonics patterns helps children with decoding by familiarizing them with common letter(s)-sound pairings. Some common phonics pattern types are:

- Long vowel sounds (the "a" in "ate," "rake," "shade")
- Short vowel sounds (the "i" in "hit," "tip," "crib")
- The long ("moon") and short ("good") "oo" sound
- Digraphs- two consonants together that make a new sound (the "ph" in "photo")
- Consonant blends- combination consonant sounds (the "ft" in "gift")
- Hard and soft c and g sounds

Phonological awareness is a broad emergent literacy skill that involves the understanding that language is made up of sound units (i.e. words, syllables, onsets, rhymes, etc.) and the ability to manipulate those units.

Fundamental phonological awareness skills:

- **Rhyming**- having an ending sound that corresponds with another (e.g. *cat, hat*)
- **Alliteration**- having the same beginning sound
- **Segmenting**- the ability to break a word up into its individual component sounds
- **Blending**- combining sounds to form words

Helping students understand phonemes and develop the ability to manipulate them is essential to their early literacy development. Some of the exercises with phonemes that are helpful for literacy development are:

- Using music, nursery rhymes, or other memorable jingles to introduce children to sounds, rhyming, and the rhythms and patterns of speech
- Phoneme isolation- recognizing separate phonemes in words
- Phoneme segmentation- separating a word into all of its phonemes
- Phoneme identification- finding common phonemes among different words
- Phoneme blending- giving a sequence of phonemes that create a word
- Phoneme addition- making a new word by adding a phoneme to an existing word
- Phoneme deletion- removing a phoneme from a word to make a new word
- Phoneme substitution- replacing a phoneme with another to form a new word

Morphology

Morphology is the study of morphemes, which are the smallest units of sound that have meaning. These can include roots, prefixes, and suffixes. Students with a knowledge of morphemes and their meanings are better equipped to decode and decipher the meaning of new words. Instruction in morphemes gives students an important tool for the structural analysis of words.

Syntax

An essential component of the conventions of written English is syntax. **Syntax** is the manner in which words are arranged into sentences in compliance with grammatical rules. Syntax is explored in more depth in the "Grammar and Conventions" section.

Semantics

Semantics is the branch of linguistics concerned with the meaning of words. Examining semantics is essential for students' vocabulary acquisition.

Vocabulary acquisition is an important part of literacy development. As readers mature, they should gain a more extensive vocabulary. There are several tools that can help students to interpret new vocabulary:

- **Affixes**- common beginnings (prefixes) and endings (suffixes) that add meaning to a base word. Understanding the meaning of an affix can help students make sense of the word.

Common Prefixes	Common Suffixes
A-	*-er*
Bi-	*-est*
Tri-	*-ing*
Un-	*-ly*
Pre-	*-fy*
Non-	*-it*
Dis-	*-is*
Anti-	*-tion*

- **Root words**- the most basic form of a word that conveys meaning. Many words in the English language have root words from other languages, such as Greek and Latin. There are hundreds of root words in the English language but a few examples are listed in the chart below.

Root Word	Meaning	Example
Aqua	Water	Aquatic
Demo	People	Democracy
Geo	Earth	Geography
Mal	Bad	Malice
Mono	One	Monologue
Poly	Many	Polytheism
Omni	All	Omniscient
Script	Write	Manuscript

- **Context clues**- information in the text surrounding a new word that help provide meaning

Grammar and Conventions

The main components of written language are grammar, usage, and syntax. **Grammar** is the set of guidelines which govern the proper use of language. **Usage** refers to the proper use of words. **Syntax** is the manner in which words are arranged into sentences.

Parts of Speech

The basic types of words which make up the English language are known as parts of speech.

Part of Speech	**Definition**	**Examples**
Noun	Person, place, thing, or idea	boy, ball, Utah, democracy
Pronoun	Word that can take the place of a noun	he, it, something
Verb	Word that reflects an action or state of being	run, be
Adverb	A word that modifies a verb	quickly, very
Adjective	Descriptive word	happy, cold
Preposition	A word that indicates direction or position, or connects two ideas	on, off, above, to, of, from, at
Article	A word that comes before a noun that indicates whether the noun is specific or non-specific	a, an, the, this
Conjunction	A words that joins two words or phrases	for, and, nor, but, or, yet, so

Nouns

There are several different ways to classify nouns.

- Common vs. Proper
    - **Common noun**- general thing or idea; does not require capitalization.

      Examples: girl, country, religion
    - **Proper noun**- refers to a specific person, place, thing, or idea and DOES require capitalization.

      Examples: Alicia, Canada, Buddhism

- Singular vs. Plural
    - **Singular**- refers to only one thing. Examples: apple, goose
    - **Plural**- refers to more than one thing. Examples: apples, geese

- Subject vs. Object
    - The **subject** of a sentence is who or what the sentence is about. The subject performs the main verb of the sentence.
    - The **object** of a sentence is not the main subject of the sentence and has the verb *performed on it*.

      Example: *"Lisa enjoys listening to music."* In this sentence, "Lisa" is the subject and "music" is the object.

- Concrete vs. Abstract
    - **Concrete noun**- physical object. Examples: rock, building
    - **Abstract noun-** non-physical things, like ideas. Examples: creativity, sadness

Pronouns

Pronouns take the place of more specific nouns. The noun that a pronoun stands for is called the **antecedent.**

Example: *"Daniel works as a financial planner. He has worked at the same company for ten years."*

In this example, "he" is the pronoun and "Daniel" is the antecedent.

Just like nouns, pronouns can be classified as subjects or objects.

- Subject pronouns: he, she, I, we, they
- Object pronouns: him, her, me, us, them

Pronouns can also show possession.

- Examples: her, his, my, mine, ours, their

Verbs

There are three major types of verbs—action, linking, and helping.

- **Action verbs** show an action performed by the subject of a sentence.
  - Example: She ran to the store.

- **Linking verbs** connect the subject of the sentence to the additional information about the subject.
  - Example: The cat was black.

- **Helping verbs** are paired with another verb and are often used to indicate tense.
  - Example: School will be open tomorrow.

Verbs also indicate the time period in which the action is taking place. This is called **tense**. There are three major tenses—present, past, and future.

- **Present tense**- the action is occurring now

  Example: Anna lives in New York City.

- **Past tense**- the action occurred in the past

  Example: Anna lived in New York City.

- **Future tense**- the action will occur in the future

  Example: Anna will live in New York City.

Syntax

Syntax is the manner in which words are arranged into sentences. There are rules that govern proper syntax. A sentence must contain both a subject and a predicate.

- **Subject-** the part of the sentence that is *performing* the action; the noun that the sentence is about

  Example: Many trees and bushes grow in the forest.

- **Predicate-** gives information about the subject

  Example: Many trees and bushes grow in the forest.

A sentence *may* also contain one or more objects. As stated above, an object is a noun that receives the action of the verb. Objects can be direct or indirect.

- **Direct object-** directly receives the action of the predicate; answer the questions "whom?" or "what?"

- **Indirect object**- indirectly receives the action of the predicate; answer the questions "to whom/what?" "from whom/what?"

- Example: *"I gave a treat to the dog."*

  Subject- "I"

  Direct object- "treat"

  Indirect object- "dog"

Words are grouped together in several basic forms.

- **Phrases** are the most basic grouping of words. The words are related but may lack a subject (e.g. "went swimming) and/or a predicate (e.g. "my mother").

- **Clauses** are groups of words that contain both a subject and a verb. There are two types of clauses:
  - **Independent clause**- expresses a complete thought and could stand alone as a complete sentence
  - **Dependent clause**- does not express a complete thought and therefore could not stand alone as a complete sentence
  - Example: *"Because he got a flat tire, Tim was late to work."*

    "Tim was late to work" is an independent clause because it could stand alone as a complete sentence.

    "Because he got a flat tire" is a dependent clause because it could not stand alone as a complete sentence.

- **Sentences** are groups of words that contain both a subject and a predicate and express a complete thought.

Types of Sentences

A **sentence** is a grammatical structure that includes both a subject and a predicate and expresses a complete thought.

There are four main types of sentences:

1. **Declarative-** makes a statement and ends with a period.
   Example: My dog's name is Bruno.

2. **Imperative-** gives a command and usually ends with a period.
   Example: Give me that pencil.

3. **Interrogative-** asks a question and ends with a question mark.
   Example: Will you eat dinner with us tonight?

4. **Exclamatory-** shows strong feeling and ends with an exclamation point.
   Example: I'm so happy to see you!

Sentence Structure

There are four main types of sentence structures:

- **Simple sentences** contain one independent clause.
  Example: I went to the store.

- **Compound sentences** contain two or more independent clauses, joined by a conjunction or punctuation mark.
  Example: I went to the store and I bought eggs.

- **Complex sentences** contain one independent clause and at least one dependent clause.
  Example: On my way home from work, I went to the store.

- **Compound-complex sentences** contain at least two independent clauses and at least one dependent clause.
  Example: On my way home from work, I went to the store and I bought eggs, then I stopped for gas.

Works of Literature and Literary Analysis

Teachers should be familiar with the major works of literature from the United States and around the world, and should be knowledgeable of the components and techniques of literary analysis and criticism.

Topics Addressed:

1. American Literature
2. World Literature
3. Literary Analysis and Criticism

Each period of history in the United States has had its own set of culturally significant works of literature. Some of these works are listed below.

Colonial Era Literature (16th-18th centuries)

In Colonial America, literature tended to deal with several major themes, including survival, the relationship between humans and nature, and spirituality. During the Revolutionary, literature followed the politics of the time and was largely concerned with issues of rights, government, liberty, and the future of the nation.

Major works from the colonial period include:

- *The Mayflower Compact*- agreement written by those aboard the Mayflower about how they would set up their society
- The poetry of Anne Bradstreet, concerned with community, relationships, and spirituality
- *The Declaration of Independence* written primarily by Thomas Jefferson, proclaiming the status of the United States as a nation independent from Great Britain
- *Common Sense* by Thomas Paine encouraged Americans to join the cause of the Revolution

Early 19th Century Literature

In the time before the Civil War, works concerning American history tended to be idealistic in nature, presenting the new nation and its heroes in a glorious light. Two major movements during this time period were romanticism and transcendentalism. Romanticism was a s within literature and the arts which emphasized human emotion. Transcendentalism was a religious and philosophical movement that emphasized self-reliance, peaceful living, and harmony with nature.

Major works from this period include:

- American folktales, including the works of James Fennimore Cooper and Washington Irving

- Oliver Wendell Holmes ("Old Ironsides") and Henry Wadsworth Longfellow ("Paul Revere's Ride") were among the "Fireside Poets" whose poetry was considered conventional and family-friendly (it could be read together by the fire as a family in winter).
- *The Scarlett Letter*, a novel by Nathaniel Hawthorne, is an examination of morality in Puritanical New England
- Herman Melville's *Moby Dick* about a sea captain's encounter with a whale is a classic of American literature.
- The poetry and novels of Edgar Allen Poe ("The Raven," *The Fall of the House of Usher*) showed the darker side of romanticism.
- Major transcendentalist writers included Henry David Thoreau (*Walden*) and Ralph Waldo Emerson (*Nature*).

Mid to Late 19th Century

The events of the mid- to late 19th century had a dramatic effect on literature. The Civil War, Reconstruction, westward expansion, and industrialization all profoundly changed American society and along with it, American literature. As America expanded westward, a common theme in literature became tales of life on the frontier. This included both "tall tales" of heroes and more realistic portrayals of survival in the western territories.

Another literacy movement in this period was realism. As a result of the harsh realities of life introduced by the Civil War and industrialization, authors and artists began to reject the idealistic portrayals of life found in romanticism and instead show life as it is, hardships and all. This became known as realism.

Major works from this period include:

- The poetry of Walt Whitman and Emily Dickenson
- *Uncle Tom's Cabin* by Harriet Beecher Stowe helped to shed light on the issue of slavery
- *The Red Badge of Courage* by Stephen Crane, which depicted the life of Civil War soldiers
- Tall tales of heroes such as Paul Bunyan and Pecos Bill
- The novels of Mark Twain, including *The Adventures of Tom Sawyer* and *The Adventures of Huckleberry Finn*, which depicted life along the Mississippi

- The novels of Henry James, an American who spent many years living in England, which explore the differences between the Old World and the New World.

20th Century

The literature of the 20th century explored a wide array of themes. The harsh realities of industrialization, two World Wars, and the Great Depression caused many authors to write about disillusionment with the world.

Major works from this period include:

- *The Jungle* by Upton Sinclair, which exposed harsh and unsanitary conditions within the meatpacking industry and helped to prompt industrial reform
- The poetry of T.S. Eliot, Ezra Pound, and Robert Frost
- Ernest Hemingway, who wrote largely of World War I in novels such as *A Farewell to Arms*
- Novels by F. Scott Fitzgerald, including *The Great Gatsby*, which explore themes of excessive consumerism and the emptiness behind the apparent glamour of the "Roaring '20s"
- Edith Wharton's writing, including *The Age of Innocence*, criticize upper-class society
- John Steinbeck's works, including *The Grapes of Wrath, East of Eden,* and *Of Mice and Men*, depicted life in the Great Depression
- Harper Lee's *To Kill a Mockingbird* deals with issues of racism and justice

World Literature

This section provides an overview of classical and contemporary literature from around the world. It is by no means an extensive list, but rather lists a sampling of works that are considered to be among the most famous and influential from their areas of origin.

British Literature

The United Kingdom has a long literary history that has produced many of the classics of the Western world.

Major authors and works from the United Kingdom include:

- *Beowulf*, the first English epic, written anonymously
- Geoffrey Chaucer (*The Canterbury Tales*)
- The plays and poetry of William Shakespeare
- Jane Austen (*Pride and Prejudice, Sense and Sensibility*)
- Emily Bronte (*Wuthering Heights*)
- Charlotte Bronte (*Jane Eyre*)
- George Eliot (*Silas Marner*)
- Charles Dickens (*Great Expectations, A Tale of Two Cities*)
- Poets including Samuel Taylor Coleridge, William Wordsworth, John Keats, and Lord Byron
- Thomas Hobbes (*Leviathan*)
- John Locke (*Two Treatises on Government*)

Continental European Literature

Continental Europe has also produced great works on literature in a variety of languages. Some of the major authors and their works are listed on the follow pages.

Austria

- Franz Kafka (*The Metamorphosis*)

France

- Alexandre Dumas *(The Three Musketeers; The Count of Monte Cristo*)
- Moliere (plays, including *The Misanthrope*)
- Victor Hugo (*Les Miserables, The Hunchback of Notre Dame*)
- Jean Jacques Rousseau (*The Social Contract*)
- Voltaire (*Candide*)
- Baron de Montesquieu (*Confessions*)
- Marcel Proust (*In Search of Lost Time*)

Germany

- Johann Wolfgang von Goethe (*Faust*)
- Friedrich Stiller (*Wallenstein*)
- Heinrich Ibsen (*A Doll's House*)
- Anne Frank (*Diary of a Young Girl*)

Greece

- Homer (*The Odyssey, The Iliad*)
- The writings of classical philosophers such as Socrates, Plato, and Aristotle
- The plays of ancient Greek dramatists such as Euripides and Sophocles

Italy

- Francesco Petrarch (poetry)
- Virgil (*The Aenied*)
- Dante Alighieri (*The Diving Comedy*)
- Niccolo Machiavelli (*The Prince*)

Romania

- Elie Wiesel (*Night*)

Russia

- Leo Tolstoy (*War and Peace, Anna Karenina*)
- Fyodor Dostoevsky (*Crime and Punishment, The Brothers Karamazov*)
- Anton Chekhov (*The Cherry Orchard*)

Spain

- Miguel de Cervantes (*Don Quixote*)
- Juan Roman Jimenez (poetry)

Asian Literature

The Asian continent is the largest in the world and its people are very diverse. Asian cultures have a rich literary history that spans thousands of years, as well as many nations, languages, and faiths. Some of the major authors and works are listed below.

China

- Confucius (*The Analects*)
- Laozi (*Dao de Jing*)
- Sun Tzu (*The Art of War*)
- Li Po, or Li Bai (poetry)

India

- *The Vedas,* an early religious text sacred to the Hindus
- Early epics written in Sanskrit, including *Ramayana* and *Mahabharata*
- Rabindranath Tagore (*Song Offerings*)
- Mahatma Gandhi (*The Story of My Experiments with the Truth*, *Hind Swaraj*)

Japan

- *The Tale of Genji* by Murasaki Shikibu, considered the world's first novel
- Japanese drama including the kabuki and Noh styles
- Haiku poetry
- Fumiko Hayashi (*Drifting Clouds*)

Middle East

- The sacred text of several major religions originated in the Middle East, including the Bible (Christianity), the Qur'an (Islam), and the Torah and Talmud (Judaism).
- *One Thousand and One Nights*, a collection of Arabic folktales
- *Rihla*, which documents the travels of explorer Ibn Battuta

Latin American Literature

Latin American literature has been significantly influenced by Spanish, Portuguese, other European, and indigenous cultures that blended during the settlement of these areas.

Major authors and words from Latin America include:

- Gabriel Garcia Marquez (*One Hundred Years of Solitude*)
- Octavio Paz (*The Labyrinth of Solitude*)
- Pablo Neruda (poetry)
- Jorge Luis Borges (*Ficciones*)
- Gabriela Mistral (poetry)
- Carlos Fuentes (*Terra Nostra*)

African Literature

Africa has a long and rich history of oral literature, which consists mainly of mythological and historical tales passed down through the generations. Additionally, its written literature includes the authors and works listed below.

- A famous example of oral literature is *The Epic of Sundiata* about the founder of the Mali Empire, which dates from the 14th century
- Writings of political leaders such as Nelson Mandela (*Long Walk to Freedom*)
- Chinua Achebe (*Things Fall Apart*)
- Peter Abrahams (*Tell Freedom: Memories of Africa*)

Elements of Literary Analysis

Literary analysis goes beyond the retelling of a story and instead involves a presentation of the reader's interpretation of a piece of literature. When analyzing a work of literature, it is essential to give attention to the major story elements including:

- Setting
- The types and functions of characters
- Point of view
- Conflict
- Theme
- Style

These elements of storytelling will be explored in further detail in the sections that follow.

Focuses of Literary Criticism

Literary criticism involves the evaluation of works of literature. There are several major types of literary criticism, each with their own points of focus:

1. Biographical Criticism- uses knowledge of the author's life to frame the criticism of the work
2. Formalist Criticism- focuses of the form of the writing
3. Historical Criticism- focuses on the historical context in which the piece was written
4. Psychological Criticism- applies the tools of psychology to the author and/or the characters in the piece to try to understand their motivations
5. Reader-Response Criticism- focuses on what happens in the reader's mind as he or she interprets the text

Literary Genres, Elements, and Techniques

This section covers the major types of literature and the literary devices and structures that comprise them.

Topics Addressed:

1. Literary Terms
2. Types of Literature
3. Elements of Non-Fiction
4. Elements of Fiction
5. Elements of Poetry
6. Elements of Drama

Literary Terms

Literature employs devices to convey meaning through the written word.

Term	Definition	Example
Alliteration	Repetition of a beginning consonant sound	The lonesome lady left one last, long, look for her love.
Flashback	An interruption in the chronology of a story that takes the narrative back in time from its current point	The novel *Frankenstein* by Mary Shelley is told largely in flashbacks as Dr. Frankenstein recounts his story for a sea captain.
Foreshadowing	An advanced warning or clue as to what is to come later in a story	The witches in Shakespeare's *Macbeth* foreshadow the events to come.
Hyperbole	Exaggeration for emphasis	I'm so hungry I could eat a whole elephant!
Idiom	A phrase that has come to have a different meaning through usage than the meanings of its individual words	Something easy is said to be "a piece of cake."
Imagery	Descriptive writing that appeals to the senses	The rich aroma of coffee drifted through the air, bringing warmth on a bitter January morning.
Metaphor	A comparison between two things that does not use "like" or "as"	He is a chicken.
Onomatopoeia	Words that convey sounds	Buzz, crackle, pop, bang
Oxymoron	Combining two words with opposite meanings	Jumbo shrimp
Personification	Giving human characteristics to nonhuman things	The leaves danced as the wind whistled through the trees.
Simile	A comparison between two things that uses "like" or "as"	Cool as a cucumber

Types of Literature

There are many types of literature. They fall under two general categories—fiction and non-fiction. **Fiction** is material that not an accurate account of real people and events but rather is imagined by the author. **Non-fiction** is material that is presented as being factual and accurate.

The major forms of fiction and non-fiction literature include, but are not limited to, those listed in the chart that follows:

Fiction	Non-Fiction
• Drama (play)- a piece meant for performance, where the story is presented through dialogue • Novel- a book-length narrative that presents its characters and plot with a degree of realism • Poetry- literature written in verse • Short story- a brief work of narrative prose	• Autobiography- an account of the author's own life • Biography- an account of another person's life • Diary (or journal)- a dated, personal record of events over a period of time • Essay- a short piece intended to express an author's point of view on a topic • Letter- written correspondence from one person to another • Textbook-a book used to study a particular subject

Types of Non-Fiction

Non-fiction writing can be classified as informational, persuasive, or functional.

Informational texts are meant to teach the reader facts about a subject.

Examples:

- Biography or autobiography
- Textbook
- Encyclopedia

Persuasive texts are meant to convince the audience of a point of view.

Examples:

- Editorial
- Persuasive essay

Functional texts provide instructions for the reader.

Examples:

- How-to guide
- Instruction manual

Structures of Non-Fiction Texts

Informational (non-fiction) texts typically have structural components that can help students to comprehend the material and to locate specific information they need. These structural features may include:

- Table of contents
- Glossary
- Index
- Bibliography
- Headings
- Outlines
- Key terms underlined or in bold print
- Graphic components such as illustrations, photographs, charts, graphs, or tables

Teaching students about these textual features can help them to better understand the information presented in the text. These structures are in place to help the reader to summarize and synthesize the information. Some techniques for familiarizing students with these structures are:

- Having students preview these features of the text before reading
- Having a text "scavenger hunt" to locate text features
- Using these features (especially headings and key terms) as the basis for outlines or graphic organizers

Elements of Fiction

The major elements of fiction include setting, theme, plot, character, and point of view.

Setting

The setting is when and where the story takes place. This can be a real or imagined place and time period. The setting is introduced earlier in the story.

Theme

The theme is the underlying idea of a story. A theme may be a message the author is trying to convey, a lesson learned by a character in the story, or a universal truth.

Plot

The plot is made up of the events in the story. There are five parts to a plot:

1. Introduction- the characters, setting, and necessary background information are introduced
2. Rising action- the story becomes more complex and the conflict is introduced
3. The types of conflict are *man vs. man, man vs. self, man vs. nature, man vs. society,* and *man vs. fate*.
4. Climax- the height of the conflict and turning point of the story
5. Falling action- the conflict begins to resolve itself
6. Resolution- the conflict is resolved and the story concludes

Characters

Characters are the people (or sometimes animals or objects) who participate in a story. The two main types of characters are the **protagonist** (the main character or hero) and the **antagonist** (the character that works against the protagonist).

Point of View

Point of view refers to the perspective from which the narration takes place. It addresses who is telling the story (the narrator).

Main Types of Narrators:

- First person- ones of the characters tells the story from his or her own perspective; uses "I"
- Third person- the story is told by an outside voice who is not one of the characters
- Omniscient- a third person narrator who knows everything about all of the characters, including their inner thoughts and feelings.
- Limited omniscient- a third person narrator who only knows the inner thoughts and feelings of one specific character

Elements of Poetry

Poetry is a form of creative literature written in verse.

Types of Poetry

Poetry can take many forms, several of which are listed in the chart below:

Form	Definition
Acrostic	A poem in which the first letter of each line forms a word when read from top to bottom
Ballad	A poem narrating a story in stanzas, often quatrains
Blank Verse	Poetry that is metered but not rhymed
Cinquain	A five line poem with specified syllabic emphasis, depending on the type of cinquain
Concrete	A poem written into a familiar shape relating to the poem's meaning
Elegy	A poem about someone's death
Epic	A long poem about the adventures of a hero
Free Verse	Poetry that is neither rhymed nor metered
Haiku	A Japanese form of poetry that contains three lines of 5, 7, and 5 syllables, in that order
Limerick	A humorous five-line poem with a rhyme scheme of AABBA
Lyric	A poem expressing personal emotions
Ode	A lyric poem addressed to a particular subject, which often contains lofty imagery
Sonnet	A fourteen-line poem

Poetry Terms and Devices

Poetry also has its own unique vocabulary of terms, including techniques that poets employ in creating their works. The chart on the following pages lists several of the major elements used in various forms of poetry.

<table>
<tr><th>Term</th><th>Definition</th><th>Example</th></tr>
<tr><td>Alliteration</td><td>Repetition of a beginning consonant sound</td><td>“Peter Piper picked a peck of pickled peppers.”</td></tr>
<tr><td>Assonance</td><td>Repetition of vowel sounds</td><td>“As I was going to St. Ives, I met a man with seven wives.”</td></tr>
<tr><td>Consonance</td><td>Repetition of consonant sounds anywhere in the words</td><td>“Hickory, Dickory, Dock,
The mouse ran up the clock.
The clock struck one,
The mouse ran down.
Hickory, Dickory, Dock.”</td></tr>
<tr><td>Foot</td><td>One unit of meter</td><td><table>
<tr><th>Type of Foot</th><th>Definition</th></tr>
<tr><td>Iambic</td><td>Unstressed syllable followed by a stressed syllable</td></tr>
<tr><td>Trochaic</td><td>Stressed syllable followed by an unstressed syllable</td></tr>
<tr><td>Spondaic</td><td>Two stressed syllables in a row</td></tr>
<tr><td>Pyrrhic</td><td>Two unstressed syllables in a row</td></tr>
<tr><td>Anapestic</td><td>Two unstressed syllables followed by a stressed syllable</td></tr>
<tr><td>Dactylic</td><td>Stressed syllable followed by two unstressed syllables</td></tr>
</table></td></tr>
<tr><td>Meter</td><td>The rhythm of a poem, dependent on the number of syllables and how they are accented</td><td></td></tr>
<tr><td>Mood</td><td>A poem’s feeling or atmosphere</td><td></td></tr>
<tr><td>Repetition</td><td>Using a word or phrase more than once for rhythm or emphasis</td><td>“Show men dutiful?
Why, so didst thou: seem they grave and learned?
Why, so didst thou: come they of noble family?
Why, so didst thou: seem they religious?
Why, so didst thou.”</td></tr>
</table>

<table>
<tr><th>Term</th><th>Definition</th><th>Example</th></tr>
<tr><td>Rhyme</td><td>The repetition of ending word sounds; can be internal rhyme (within a line) or end rhyme (the words at the end of the lines rhyme with each other)</td><td>Internal rhyme:
“Jack Sprat could eat no fat.”
End rhyme:
“Little Miss Muffet
Sat on a tuffet”</td></tr>
<tr><td>Rhythm</td><td>The pattern of sounds with a poem</td><td></td></tr>
<tr><td>Stanza</td><td>Groups of lines of poetry; named for how many lines they contain</td><td><table>
<tr><th>Name</th><th># of Lines</th></tr>
<tr><td>Couplet</td><td>2</td></tr>
<tr><td>Triplet</td><td>3</td></tr>
<tr><td>Quatrain</td><td>4</td></tr>
<tr><td>Quintain</td><td>5</td></tr>
<tr><td>Sestet</td><td>6</td></tr>
<tr><td>Septet</td><td>7</td></tr>
<tr><td>Octane</td><td>8</td></tr>
</table></td></tr>
<tr><td>Verse</td><td>A line of metered poetry; named for the number of feet per line</td><td><table>
<tr><th>Name</th><th># of Feet</th></tr>
<tr><td>Monometer</td><td>1</td></tr>
<tr><td>Dimeter</td><td>2</td></tr>
<tr><td>Trimeter</td><td>3</td></tr>
<tr><td>Tetrameter</td><td>4</td></tr>
<tr><td>Pentameter</td><td>5</td></tr>
<tr><td>Hexameter</td><td>6</td></tr>
<tr><td>Heptameter</td><td>7</td></tr>
<tr><td>Octometer</td><td>8</td></tr>
</table></td></tr>
</table>

Elements of Drama

A drama is a story acted out for an audience. Drama can be used in the classroom for story-telling, role playing, reenactment, or interpretation.

Story

The story of a drama contains the same basic elements as any other literary story—introduction, setting, rising action, conflict, climax, falling action, and conclusion. A drama can be about almost any subject. Two common forms of drama are comedy and tragedy. Comedies are usually light-hearted and have a happy ending. Tragedies have an unhappy ending, usually involving the downfall of a main character.

In most dramas, the story is written first before it is performed. The written form is called a script. In some cases, actors perform all or some actions and words that are not scripted. This is called improvisation.

Characters

Characters are played by actors. Just like in other forms of narrative, there is usually a protagonist and an antagonist.

Dialogue

Dialogue is how stories are told through drama. Dialogue consists of the spoken words of the actors.

Stage

The stage is the area used for performance. It may or may not be a raised area.

Sets and Costumes

Sometimes, sets and costumes are used to enhance dramas and make them more realistic for the audience. Sets are elements such as backdrops and furniture that help transform the stage space into the setting of the play. Costumes are the clothes, shoes, makeup, wigs, etc. that make the actors physically resemble their characters.

Literature for Children

There is a wide variety of literature available that is aimed at children in both its reading level and content. This literature has a variety of important uses in the classroom.

Topics Addressed:

1. Genres and Works of Children's Literature
2. Themes of Children's Literature
3. Selecting and Using Children's Literature in the Classroom

Genres and Works of Children's Literature

Literature for children is written in many different genres. The chart below shows some of the major ones, along with examples from some of the major authors and works of children's literature.

Genre	Description	Example(s)
Allegory	Story in which the characters and events represent ideas or concepts	Dr. Seuss wrote a number of allegorical books, including *Yertle the Turtle* (the rise and fall of Adolf Hitler), *The Sneetches* (discrimination), and *The Butter Battle Book* (the Cold War arms race).
Drama (play)	A piece meant for performance, where the story is presented through dialogue	Many fairy tales and other children's stories have been adapted for the stage.
Fable	A short story with a moral lesson	Aesop's Fables, such as *The Ant and the Grasshopper, The Boy who Cried Wolf,* and *The Tortoise and the Hare*
Fairy Tale	A short fantasy story (see below), typically derived from folklore	The major writers of fairy tales are Brothers Grimm of Germany and Hans Christian Anderson of Denmark.
Fantasy	Stories involving make-believe that often occur in imaginative realms with creatures or powers that do not exist in real life	• *Harry Potter* series (J.K. Rowling) • *The Chronicles of Narnia* (C.S. Lewis) • *A Wrinkle in Time* (Madeline L'Engle) • Numerous works by Roald Dahl, including *James and the Giant Peach, Charlie and the Chocolate Factory, and Matilda* • *The Phantom Tollbooth* (Norton Juster) • *Peter Pan* (J.M Barrie) • *Tuck Everlasting* (Natalie Babbitt)
Folktale	A story passed down through oral traditions	• *Stone Soup* (Marcia Brown) is based on a French folktale. • *Tikki Tikki Tembo* (Arlene Mosel) is an adaptation of a Chinese folktale. • *Why Mosquitoes Buzz in People's Ears* (Verna Aardema) is based on a West African folktale.

Genre	Description	Example(s)
Historical fiction	Story that takes place in the past and is realistic for that time period	• *Number the Stars* (Lois Lowry) • *Catherine, Called Birdy* (Karen Cushman) • *Anne of Green Gables* (L.M. Montgomery) • *Little House on the Prairie* series (Laura Ingalls Wilder) • *Sarah, Plain and Tall* (Patricia MacLachlan) • *Bud, Not Buddy* (Christopher Paul Thomas)
Myth	A story created to explain natural or social phenomena	Many of the famous tales from Greek and Roman mythology have been adapted for children.
Non-fiction	Factual information	• *Diary of a Young Girl* (Anne Frank) • *I Am...* series of biographies (Brad Meltzer)
Parable	A short story used to teach a moral lesson	• *The Little Prince*(Antoine de Saint-Exupéry) • *The Giving Tree* (Shel Silverstein)
Poetry	Stories or ideas expressed through verse	*Where the Sidewalk Ends* (poetry collection by Shel Silverstein)
Picture book	Illustrated stories where the text and pictures are interdependent	• *Where the Wild Things Are* (Maurice Sendak) • *The Very Hungry Caterpillar* (Eric Carle) • *Cloudy with a Chance of Meatballs* (Judy Barrett) • *Goodnight, Moon* (Margaret • *If You Give a Mouse a Cookie* (Laura Numeroff) • *Corduroy* (Don Freeman)
Realistic fiction	Fiction that takes place in the contemporary "real world" with characters and situations that are believable	• Books by Judy Blume, including *Tales of a Fourth Grade Nothing* and *Freckle Juice* • The *Ramona* series by Beverly Cleary
Science fiction	Story created by extending scientific ideas to imaginary, though logical, conclusions; often set in the future	• *Commander Toad* series (Jane Yolen) • The *Sixth Grade Alien* and *My Teacher is an Alien* series (Bruce Coville) • *Danny Dunn* series (Jay Williams) • *The Iron Giant* (Ted Hughes)
Tall tale	An exaggerated story, usually about a real person	American tall tales include the stories of John Henry, Pecos Bill, Paul Bunyan and Babe the Blue Ox, and Johnny Appleseed.

Themes of Children's Literature

Children's literature can cover many broad themes. Some of the most common include:

- Perseverance and overcoming obstacles
- Acceptance of differences in others
- Courage
- Cooperation with others
- The importance of family and/or friendship
- Loyalty
- Honesty
- Treating others with compassion and kindness

Many times, children's literature is aimed at teaching lessons about making moral choices. The stories are meant to be entertaining for children to read, but along the way they are also learning about integrity and proper behavior.

Selecting Developmentally Appropriate Literature

Children's authors work to create literature that is developmentally appropriate, both in reading level and in content. Children's literature is placed into categories according to development level:

- **Early Readers** are targeted for beginning readers and are typically formatted as board books or picture books. These books are usually under 50 pages in length and a have stories written in simple language and supported by illustrations.
- **Middle Grade Readers** include longer books that contain more text and fewer (if any) illustrations than early readers. These also can contain more complex information or plots and more sophisticated vocabulary than early readers. A common format for a middle grade reader is a basic chapter book.
- **Young Adult** literature is aimed at teenage audiences. These are typically longer chapter books whose stories often revolve around teenagers or issues that teenagers typically face.

Choose (or allow children to choose) books that match them both in interest and in appropriateness for their reading level. Aim to choose "just right texts" for most of their reading (rather than those that are easy or so difficult that they lead to much frustration).

Using Literature in the Classroom

Literature has a variety of uses in the classroom in addition to being used as a tool for literacy development. It can be used as resource material for research, to create cross-curricular connections between all subject areas, to foster creativity, to model good writing, to promote social development skills, and to foster cross-cultural understanding (see "Multicultural Literature" below).

Multicultural Literature

Multicultural children's literature feature a variety of cultures and ethnicities. Incorporating multicultural literature is important as it makes students of diverse backgrounds feel represented, welcomed, valued, and included. It also encourages all students to develop multicultural appreciation, sensitivity, and knowledge.

When selecting multicultural texts, it is important to keep in mind that the texts should:

- Show sensitivity
- Contain accurate portrayals of cultures
- Present cultures in a positive light
- Avoid stereotyping

Writing and Composition

In order to become effective writers, students should follow the steps of the basic writing process and learn to effectively use organizational and style elements to enhance their writing.

Topics Addressed:

1. The Writing Process
2. Formal Elements of Writing
3. Modes and Traits of Writing

The Writing Process

As students learn to write, it is important for them to learn to write according to a clear process in order to ensure that their writing is given thought and quality. Throughout the writing process, peer editing can be a valuable tool to help students evaluate and revise their work.

The Five Stages of the Writing Process:

1. **Prewriting-** generate and record ideas for writing; this can include techniques such as brainstorming, semantic mapping, outlining, and using graphic organizers
2. **Rough Draft**- write down all of the ideas in an organized way
3. **Revise-** reread the rough draft and make changes to how the information is presented and organized; make sure tone, purpose, and audience are clear; add or delete content as needed
4. **Edit**- make changes to spelling, grammar, and other mechanics
5. **Publish**- create the final copy

Formal Elements of Writing

Organization and Paragraphing

An important component of writing its organization. Writing should follow a clear and logical order, typically based either on chronology or to follow the progression of an argument.

Foundational to the organization of writing is paragraphing. Paragraphing helps to break long pieces of writing into chunks that are easier for the reader to take in. Each paragraph should contain a common theme. A new idea should prompt the beginning of a new paragraph.

A paragraph should contain a topic sentence, which introduces the idea of the paragraph. There should also be smooth and logical transitions between paragraphs (at the end of one paragraph and/or the beginning of the next) to help the reader to follow the progression of thought (see "Improving Writing Style" below for more on transitions).

Helping Students Organize Writing

Students should be taught to organize their writing in a logical, coherent manner, according to structures that make sense for the type of writing they are engaging in.

Some ways to encourage writing organization include:

- Teaching story structure and other common structures of writing
- Providing outlines
- Using graphic organizers
- Routine
- Questioning and providing feedback

Improving Writing Style

Writing style includes such components as vocabulary, word choice, and fluidity. Students should be taught these elements of writing at increasing levels of sophistication as their literacy skills develop over their educational careers.

Some important elements include:

- **Precise language**- choosing words that are specific, and thus make a clearer mental picture for the reader (e.g., "poodle" instead of "dog")

- **Figurative language**- words or phrases that have meanings other than the literal meanings of the words, used for effect (e.g., simile, metaphor, hyperbole)
- **Transitions/linking words**- words or phrases used to move from one idea to the other; can include:
  - Location (e.g., on top of, above, below, across from)
  - Time (e.g., after, before, often)
  - Comparison (e.g., as, like, likewise, also)
  - Contrast (e.g., not, but, although, however)
  - Elaboration (e.g., also, again, additionally, furthermore)
  - Emphasis (e.g., all in all, as you can see, once again)
  - Conclusion (e.g., therefore, hence, in conclusion)
- **Temporal words**- words used to indicate time (e.g., at first, later, as soon as)
- **Sensory words**- words meant to appeal to the five senses, describing the look, sound, feel, taste, and smell of things (e.g., haggard, loud, fluffy, sweet, putrid)
- **Dialogue**- direct quotations spoken by characters in the writing; students must also be taught the proper punctuation for dialogue
- **Sentence variety**- Using different types of sentences structures makes writing more interesting for the reader.

Modes and Traits of Writing

Modes of Writing

There are six main modes of writing elementary students may encounter:

1. **Expositor/Informational Writing:** writing meant to instruct or explain

   Examples: research papers, reports, biographies

2. **Narrative Writing:** writing that tells a story

   Examples: novels, short stories, plays

3. **Persuasive Writing:** writing that expresses the author's point of view

   Examples: argumentative essay, editorial, reviews, advertisements

4. **Journaling/Letter Writing:** writing written as a personal message for a specific audience (either themselves or another person or organization)

   Examples: journals/diaries, learning logs, business letters, personal letters, emails

5. **Descriptive Writing:** writing meant to describe someone or something; uses language that appeals to the senses

   Examples: descriptive essays, character sketches

6. **Creative Writing:** writing drawn from the author's imagination

   Examples: fiction, poetry

Traits of Writing

All writing contains three main traits—tone, purpose, and audience. Keeping these in mind while writing and being intentional about the message you want to present is the best way to write effectively.

- **Tone-** the feeling or attitude that a piece of writing conveys

  Examples: humorous, sad, serious, uplifting

  Ensure that the tone is clear and appropriate for what you are trying to accomplish with the piece of writing.

- **Purpose-** why the author wrote the piece; what is the goal of this piece of writing?

  Examples: to persuade, to entertain, to inform, to instruct

  Keep this purpose in mind throughout to maintain focus of the goal of the writing. This will help to inform tone and language choices.

- **Audience-** who the piece is intended for; who is supposed to be reading this?

  Examples: children, adults, women, sports fans

  Ensure that the reading level and writing style are appropriate for that audience.

Organizational Structures of Writing

Writing can take on many forms and be organized in many ways. Structures of writing are devices that help the writing to accomplish its purpose. Some examples of writing structures are:

- **Description**- a writing mode for creating a mental picture of someone or something
- **Definition**- provides a statement of the exact meaning of something
- **Argument**- presents a case in favor of a particular point of view or opinion
- **Examples**- provide evidence to clarify an idea, add details, or to give support to an argument

The organization of a piece can help the writing to fulfill its purpose by conveying meaning in the most effective manner. Some common organizational structures of writing are:

Term	Definition
Descriptive	Provides a detailed description of someone or something
Comparison/Contrast	Examines the similarities and differences between two or more things
Cause and Effect	Presents causal relationships between a particular event or idea and those that follow it
Persuasive	Aims to convince the reader of a point of view; will include arguments and supporting evidence
Problem-Solution	Presents a problem, suggest and explains a possible solution, and discusses the potential effects of the solution
Sequential	Presents events in chronological order or presents a set of ordered steps; most common for a narrative

Techniques to Convey Meaning

Some important elements of writing used to help convey meaning include:

- **Precise language**- choosing words that are specific, and thus make a clearer mental picture for the reader (e.g., "poodle" instead of "dog")
- **Figurative language**- words or phrases that have meanings other than the literal meanings of the words, used for effect (e.g., simile, metaphor, hyperbole)
- **Temporal words**- words used to indicate time (e.g., at first, later, as soon as)
- **Sensory words**- words meant to appeal to the five senses, describing the look, sound, feel, taste, and smell of things (e.g., haggard, loud, fluffy, sweet, putrid)
- **Dialogue**- direct quotations spoken by characters in the writing; students must also be taught the proper punctuation for dialogue
- **Sentence variety**- Using different types of sentences structures makes writing more interesting for the reader.

History and Social Science

Social Science introduces students to topics in history, geography, government, civics, and economics in an effort to equip them to become informed and contributing members of a democratic society.

Test Structure

The History and Social Science section makes up 30% of the Multi-Subject subtest. Within History and Social Science, there are four major subcategories with which you must be familiar:

A. United States and Massachusetts History

B. Government and Economics

C. World History

D. Geography

Each subcategory is divided into topics, which state the skills you must be able to demonstrate on the exam.

United States and Massachusetts History

Students should have an understanding of the causes and effects of the major events in the history of the United States and Massachusetts.

Topics Addressed:

1. The Pre-Colonial Era
2. European Exploration
3. From Colonies to a New Nation
4. U.S. Expansion
5. Civil War and Reconstruction
6. Industrialization
7. World Wars I and II
8. The Post-World War II Era

The Pre-Colonial Era

Prior to the arrival of European explorers beginning in the fifteenth century, North America was inhabited by diverse indigenous populations. The North American landscape is diverse, including areas of plains, desert, and mountains, and those different environments resulted in vastly different Native American cultural groups across the continent.

Depending on their environment, some tribes used agriculture, growing important crops such as maize (corn), potatoes, and squash, while others relied on hunting and gathering. Tribes living in coastal areas relied more heavily on fishing.

Native American groups typically had traditional economies based on bartering. Instead of using money, goods would be exchanged directly for other goods. Trade between tribes was common as a way to obtain needed supplies.

There are numerous indigenous groups that existed (many of whom still exist, albeit usually relocated) throughout North America. Two major groups were the Iroquois and the Pueblo.

The Iroquois were not a single tribe, but rather an organized confederation of five original nations—Cayuga, Onondaga, Seneca, Oneida, and Mohawk. The Tuscarora joined the confederacy later. Today, the Iroquois are known as the Six Nations. The Iroquois originated in the American Northeast, largely in what is now New York. They are noted for their organized government and the cooperation among their nations.

The Pueblo lived in the American Southwest. The Pueblo elected a chief (rather than it being a strictly hereditary office, as was common elsewhere), making them one of the earliest representative governments in the world. The Pueblo are also noted for the way in which they adapted to their environment by creating houses and other buildings both from adobe mud-bricks and in the faces of cliffs.

Tribes native to what is now Massachusetts include the Mohegan, the Mohican, and the Wampanoag.

European Exploration

Starting in the 1400s, European powers began to look to expand their influence outward. They sent explorers to find new trade routes and new lands that could be used for their natural resources. During this period, European explorers learned about the existence of the North and South American continents and began to colonize these areas, which were collectively called the New World. Part of this territory would one day become the United States.

The three main motivations for exploration of the New World were:

- Glory- the desire for personal status and to bring prestige to the home country
- God- convert native populations to Christianity
- Gold- get riches for themselves and natural resources, new trade routes, and trading partners for the home country

Students should be familiar with some of the major explorers who navigated the Americas.

Explorer	Nation	Achievements
John Cabot	Britain	Explored the east coast of Canada
Christopher Columbus	Italy, sailed for Spain	"Discovered" North America while looking for a western route to India
Amerigo Vespucci	Italy	The first to realize the Americas were not part of Asia; America is named after him
Vasco de Balboa	Spain	First to reach the Pacific by crossing Central America
Juan Ponce de Leon	Spain	First to explore Florida while searching for the Fountain of Youth
Ferdinand Magellan	Spain	First to circumnavigate the globe by sailing around the southern tip of South America
Hernan Cortez	Spain	Conquered Mexico from the Aztecs
Francisco Pizzaro	Spain	Conquered the Incan Empire
Jacques Cartier	France	Explored Canada and claimed it for France
Fernando de Soto	Spain	Discovered the Mississippi River
Francisco Coronado	Spain	Explored the American southwest
Walter Raleigh	Britain	Established English colonies in North America
Henry Hudson	Britain	Explored northeastern North America and the Arctic
James Cook	Britain	Explored the Pacific; discovered Hawaii

The Thirteen Colonies

The British established thirteen colonies along the east coast of what is now the United States. Within the Thirteen Colonies, there were three main regions—New England, Middle Atlantic, and the Southern Colonies. Each area developed its own unique characteristics.

Region	Colonies	Characteristics
New England Colonies	New Hampshire, Massachusetts, Rhode Island, Connecticut	• Rocky soil was poor for farming • Relied on fishing and shipping industries • Most people lived in or near towns • Major city: Boston
Middle Atlantic Colonies	New York, New Jersey, Pennsylvania, Delaware	• Good conditions for farming • The "breadbasket" of the colonies • Fur trade • Major city: Philadelphia
Southern Colonies	Maryland, Virginia, North Carolina, South Carolina, Georgia	• Plantation farming (tobacco, indigo, rice, cotton) • Slavery • More rural population • Major cities: Richmond, Charleston

After the American Revolution, these colonies would become the first thirteen states. They served as the foundation for a nation that would eventually grow to include fifty states across a vast expanse of territory.

The American Revolution and the Founding of the United States

The Thirteen Colonies eventually wanted to rule themselves rather than continue to be controlled by Great Britain. This resulted in the American Revolution.

Causes of the American Revolution

When the colonies were first settled, they relied heavily on help from the British. They needed British supplies, British money, the British government to keep order, and the British military for protection. Over time, as the colonies grew more established and stronger, they became more self-sufficient. They no longer relied on the British for everything. They even made their own local governments to make decisions. The less they depended on the British, the more they felt like they didn't need them anymore and that they could govern themselves.

In the late 1700s, the British found themselves in need of money after the costly French and Indian War, so they began to impose many new taxes on the colonists. These included:

- Stamp Act (1765)
- Townshend Acts (1767)
- Tea Act (1773)
- Intolerable Acts (1774)

The colonists did not have representation in the British Parliament, which levied the taxes, so they didn't think it was fair that they should be taxed. After failed attempts at negotiation and compromise, tensions escalated and eventually erupted into war—the American Revolution.

Boston, Massachusetts played an important role in the events leading up to the American Revolution. The **Boston Massacre** (1770) in which British soldiers killed five colonial protestors further inflamed colonists against the British. The **Boston Tea Party** (1773) occurred when colonists protested the aforementioned taxes by boarding a ship and dumping tea into Boston Harbor. The Intolerable Acts were largely a response to the Boston Tea Party and included provisions designed to punish Boston specifically, including the closing of Boston Harbor.

Major Events in the American Revolution

The **American Revolution** began in Massachusetts with the **Battle of Lexington and Concord** in 1775. This was soon followed by the **Battle of Bunker Hill**.

The next summer, representatives from the colonies signed a document called the **Declaration of Independence**, which listed the reasons for the rebellion and stated that the United States was to be an independent country. It was signed on July 4, 1776.

Britain was not ready to accept American independence, however, and the war continued. While the British army was more established, better trained, and had larger numbers, the Americans had the advantage of fighting on their own familiar territory and eventually secured aid from the French. The Americans won the war with a final victory at the **Battle of Yorktown** in 1781. The war officially concluded with the signing of the Treaty of Paris in 1783.

Forming a New Nation

The new nation had to create a government for itself. The first system they tried was organized around a document called the **Articles of Confederation**. This made the new government too weak, however, and it ultimately failed.

In 1787, the Articles of Confederation were replaced with a new form of government, outlined in the **U.S. Constitution**. The Constitution set up a federal system with a three-branch national government. Revolutionary War hero George Washington was chosen as the first President of the United States.

U.S. Expansion

Over the course of its history, the United States made several major expansions, enlarging its land from thirteen original states to the current fifty.

The British had holdings in North America other than the Thirteen Colonies. Part of this was in Canada, and remained in British hands following the American Revolution. Some of this territory was adjacent to the Thirteen Colonies and became a part of the new United States. Originally, the Thirteen Colonies turned into the first thirteen states of the United States. The additional territory, which included lands between the Appalachian Mountains and the Mississippi River, was eventually settled. The territories each eventually applied for statehood and became Ohio, Indiana, Illinois, Alabama, Mississippi, Michigan, and Wisconsin.

The next major territorial expansion of the United States occurred in 1803 when President Thomas Jefferson bought the Louisiana Territory from France. The  **Louisiana Purchase** doubled the size of the nation, adding what would eventually become Louisiana, Arkansas, Missouri, Iowa, Minnesota, North Dakota, South Dakota, Kansas, Nebraska, Oklahoma, Colorado, Wyoming, and Montana.

This major expansion gave birth to the idea that the United States should one day possess the lands all the way to the Pacific Ocean. The belief that this was the nation's God-given right became known as **Manifest Destiny**. Fueled by this spirit, the nation continued to expand.

The United States purchased Florida from Spain in 1819. In 1845, it annexed Texas, which was at the time an independent republic. The Oregon Territory was acquired in 1846. The **Mexican Cession** of 1848, which followed the Mexican-American War, resulted in the acquisition of the territories that would become California, Nevada, New Mexico, Arizona, and Utah. The **Gadsden Purchase** (1853, from Mexico) completed the territories of Arizona and New Mexico. Alaska was purchased from Russia in 1867 and Hawaii was annexed in 1898.

Civil War and Reconstruction

The young nation soon became divided over the issue of slavery. States in the South permitted slavery while those in the North did not. The interests of the two regions were relatively balanced in Congress until new states started to be added in the western territories. Pro- and anti-slavery supporters each feared losing power in Congress and fought for the new states to join their side.

Eventually, the conflict escalated and the South seceded (left) the Union, forming the Confederate States of America. The United States, led by President Abraham Lincoln, did not accept the secession and fought the **Civil War** (1861-1865) in order to preserve the unity of the nation. In the end, the North won, the nation was reunited, and slavery was abolished with the passage of the **13th Amendment**.

The period following the Civil War was known as **Reconstruction**. During this period, the government worked to rebuild the South, which had been devastated by the war. Methods used during Reconstruction were controversial and led to continued resentment by many southerners. Following Reconstruction, African Americans, now free from slavery, found themselves subject to legal discrimination in the South, including segregation and voting restrictions. Many migrated to cities in the North.

Industrialization

In the mid-1800s, the United States became part of an international phenomenon known as the Industrial Revolution. During this period, rapid advancements were made in technology that allowed for production to change over from cottage industries to factory systems. This allowed for mass-production of goods.

The impact of the Industrial Revolution was far-reaching. Goods could now be manufactured quickly and cheaply. This led to great economic growth for the United States. Factories provided new jobs for many people, including the nation's large influx of immigrants, many of whom were drawn to the United States during this period because of the political freedoms and economic opportunities the country had to offer. All of those factory jobs also drew people into cities, leading to widespread urbanization. It also led to the homogenization of culture as people across the nation were able to access and afford the same goods. Technologies produced during the Industrial Revolution would shape the modern world.

Some negative effects of the Industrial Revolution included hazardous working conditions in factories, poor living conditions in crowded urban areas, and pollution. The Progressive Movement of the early 20th century, led by President Teddy Roosevelt, sought to put in place regulations to help solve some of these problems, including anti-monopoly laws, new economic rules and environmental regulations.

World War I

Though it initially sought neutrality, the United States became involved in World War I (1914-1918) in 1917 due to a combination of factors, including the Germans' use of unrestricted submarine warfare, the sinking of the *Lusitania*, and the Zimmerman Telegram.

The United States joined on the side of the Allied Powers and helped lead them to victory. The war ended with the Treaty of Versailles.

The Interwar Period

Following World War I, the United States once again sought isolation from the rest of the world, not wanting to be dragged into another war. For this reason, it declined to join the newly formed League of Nations.

The 1920s saw a period of economic prosperity for the United States. The decade became known as the **Roaring Twenties**. Economically, it was marked by mass consumerism, buying on credit, and the growth of the power of the stock market. Socially, this was the period when women gained the right to vote, when the automobile became popular, and when jazz music came to be.

The high period of the 1920s came to an abrupt end in 1929, when a massive stock market crash led to the **Great Depression**. A combination of factors, including excess spending, speculation, agricultural overproduction, and buying on margin led to the economic downturn. During the Great Depression, inflation and unemployment were high, banks failed, and families throughout the nation found themselves enduring economic hardship.

President Franklin D. Roosevelt alleviated some of the suffering in the Great Depression with his **New Deal** programs, which gave the government a more active role in the economy. The Great Depression did not come to an end, however, until World War II jumpstarted the economy by providing industrial jobs and demanding a high output of military goods.

World War II

When **World War II** (1939-1945) broke out in Europe, the United States tried to remain neutral. Once again, however, it was eventually pulled into the conflict. The immediate cause of the U.S. entry into World War II was the Japanese bombing of **Pearl Harbor** in 1941.

The United States joined the war on the side of the Allies and fought both in Europe against the Germans and Italians and in Asia against the Japanese. U.S. forces were able to provide necessary reinforcement to Allied troops in Europe, securing the victory on that front. After a drawn out battle in the Pacific, the United States brought the war to a swift end with the dropping of the first **atomic bombs** on the Japanese cities of Hiroshima and Nagasaki.

The war concluded with th~~e Treaty of Paris~~. The **United Nations** was soon established as an international peacekeeping organization to replace the League of Nations. The United States joined as a prominent member.

The Cold War

Following World War II, Europe was devastated by the conflict, leaving two superpowers left on the world stage—the United States and the Soviet Union. The two nations had competing ideologies (capitalism vs. communism; individualism vs. collectivism) and both wished to spread their ideals to other nations. This led to rivalry. The conflict was greatly intensified by the fact that both sides had nuclear weapons. An attack by either would have had devastating global consequences, so the **Cold War** became decades of competition and threats without direct military conflict.

The two sides fought indirectly in two major **proxy wars**, in which each nation backed a side in a foreign civil war. The **Korean War** (1950-1953) saw communist North Korea, aided by the U.S.S.R., fight to take over South Korea, aided by the United States. The conflict ended in a ceasefire with no changes in boundaries. The **Vietnam War** (1956-1975) saw communist North Vietnam (along with communists in South Vietnam called the Viet Cong), aided by the U.S.S.R., attempt to take over South Vietnam, backed by the United States. The United States eventually withdrew from the long and unpopular war, and the North won, uniting the two territories into the single communist nation of Vietnam. The Cold War came to an end in 1991 when the Soviet Union dissolved due to internal problems.

The Post-Cold War Era

The 1990s were marked by an period of economic growth and prosperity. The decade also saw the rise of the Internet Age, which has revolutionized modern society. The United States was involved in international conflicts during the 1990s, including the Persian Gulf War and Bosnia.

The early twenty-first century has been marked domestically by an economic downturn. In foreign policy, the War on Terror (in response to terrorist attacks on September 11, 2001) has shaped more than a decade of international relations. The United States has fought in long wars in Afghanistan and in Iraq.

20th Century Developments and Transformations

Social Changes

Many important social changes occurred during the twentieth century. Two of the most significant of these were increased rights for women and for African-Americans.

The women's rights movement saw its first major national success in 1920 with the passage of the 19th Amendment, which granted women the right to vote. Another major push for women's rights occurred in the 1970s, when the National Organization led the fight for equal rights for women in all areas. This included the Equal Rights Amendment (ERA) which was passed by Congress but failed to get approval by enough states to be added to the Constitution.

African-Americans, too, fought for their rights throughout much of the twentieth century. In the time since the Civil War, African-Americans faced discrimination, violence, segregation, disenfranchisement, and unequal opportunities. The Civil Rights Movement, which really gained momentum in the 1960s, sought to change that. Some of the key leaders in the Civil Rights Movement included Martin Luther King, Jr., Malcolm X, and Rosa Parks.

Some of the major developments in the Civil Rights Movement were:

- *Brown v. Board of Education of Topeka, Kansas* (1954) desegregated public schools, saying that the principle of "separate but equal" established in the earlier case of *Plessy v. Ferguson* (1896) led to facilities and conditions that were "inherently unequal."
- The Civil Rights Act (1964) outlawed discrimination based on race.
- The Voting Rights Act (1965) outlawed literacy tests and poll taxes as voting requirements, which had previously been used in some states to keep African-Americans from voting.

Technological Advancements

Technological advancements were rapid and far-reaching in the twentieth century. The wide array of innovations has changed modern society. Below is just a small sampling of the many developments of the twentieth century that have had a lasting impact.

- Communication technology- radio, television, cellular phones, computers, the internet
- Transportation technology- automobile, airplane, space travel
- Weaponry- nuclear weapons, chemical weapons

Government and Economics

Students study the government in order to better understand the society in which they live and so that they may become informed, active citizens of the democracy. It is important for students to understand how the government operates, as well as the rights and responsibilities of the nation's citizens.

Economics is a social science concerned with how goods and services are produced, bought, and sold. Students should understand the fundamental economic principles, basic components of economic systems, and the relationship between economics and society.

Topics Addressed:

1. The Purposes, Functions, and Structures of Government
2. The Government of the United States
3. The Government of Massachusetts
4. Principles of Democracy and Citizenship
5. Economic Concepts and Systems

Governments are created to maintain order in a society and for the protection of individuals' lives, liberties, and properties. Governments establish laws in order to protect these things and to prevent conflicts among people.

Functions of Government

Regardless of the type of government, there are several functions that a government is expected to carry out. The type of government will influence how to and what extent these are enacted.

The basic functions of government are:

- Establishing laws
- Public safety
- Maintaining order
- Providing public services
- Defense
- Economic activity
- Education

Structures of Government

In order to carry out these functions, governments consist of some form and combination of the following basic structures:

- Legislature- makes the laws
- Court system- provides justice and settles disputes
- Executive-enforces the laws
- Bureaucracy- carries out the day-to-day functions of the government

The Government of the United States

The United States is considered a democratic republic. The operations of its government are outlined in the **United States Constitution**.

The basic constitutional principles include:

- **Popular sovereignty**- the right of the people to rule through voting
- **Limited government-** the government can only do the duties assigned to it by the Constitution and members of the government are not above the law
- **Federalism**- the division of power between national and state governments
- **Separation of powers**- the division of power between three branches of government
- **Checks and balances**- the ability of each branch to limit the power of the other branches
- **Flexibility**- the ability of the Constitution to adapt with the times as necessary

The Federal System

The government of the United States is a **federal system**, which means that power is divided between the national and state governments. Powers allocated to the national government (e.g. the military, warfare, interstate commerce, coining money) are called **delegated powers**. Powers that belong to the states (e.g. professional licensing, intrastate commerce, establishing schools) are called **reserved powers**. Powers that are shared by both the national and state governments (e.g. taxation, making laws, having courts) are called **concurrent powers**. Within each state, there are also local governments that make day-to-day decisions affecting their communities.

Branches of Government

At the national level, power is divided between three branches of government. This **separation of powers** ensures that no one person or group has all the power. The branches are the executive, legislative, and judicial branches. Each branch has its own responsibilities, which include **checks and balances** on the other branches.

	Executive Branch	Legislative Branch	Judicial Branch
Who?	President, Vice-President	Congress (House of Representatives and Senate)	Supreme Court
How Chosen	Elected for 4-year terms (maximum of 2 terms)	House: elected for 2-year terms Senate: elected for 6-year terms	Appointed by the President and approved by Congress; serve for life
Main Duty	Enforce the laws	Make the laws	Interpret the laws
Checks on Other Branches	• Appoints Supreme Court nominees • Can veto laws	• Must approve Supreme Court nominees • Can override presidential veto • Can impeach president or Supreme Court justices	• Can declare laws or presidential actions unconstitutional

The Electoral System

Citizens aged 18 and older are eligible to vote and must register to do so in their local district. Elections in the United States are held on the first Tuesday in November. Presidential elections are held every four years and congressional elections are held every two years. The frequency of elections for state and local officials may vary by state.

Though it is not in the Constitution, the United States has, through practice, developed into a two-party system. While there have been other major parties in the past, currently, the two major parties are the Democratic Party and the Republican Party. While other parties are allowed to run candidates, they rarely gain the support needed to win seats, especially at the national level.

For many offices, the major parties hold **primary elections** (typically in the spring preceding the general election) in which voters choose who among a pool of candidates will become the official candidate for the party. The winning candidates from each party then face off against one another in the **general election** in November. The candidate with the most votes wins the seat.

In the case of presidential elections, a special electoral body known as the **electoral college** plays an important role in the election. Following the count of the popular vote in the general election, the vote then moves to the electoral college. The electoral college is made up of representatives from each state. Each state receive a certain number of electoral votes based on its population. The candidate with the most popular votes in each state receives that state's electoral votes. The electoral votes are then tallied and it is those votes that decide the election. Typically, the nationwide popular vote and the electoral vote result in the election of the same candidate, but on rare occasions, a candidate may win the presidency without having won the popular vote by having enough electoral votes.

Amendments to the Constitution

The Constitution was intended to be flexible, allowing it to change as necessary with the times. This is why it includes a process for adding **amendments**, or changes, to the document. Currently, there are twenty-seven amendments. The first ten amendments are collectively known as the **Bill of Rights** and they outline citizens' basic rights and freedoms.

The current amendments are listed in the following chart:

The Bill of Rights	
1st	Freedoms of speech, religion, press, assembly, and petition
2nd	Right to bear arms
3rd	Protection against quartering of soldiers
4th	Protection against illegal search and seizure
5th	Right to due process; protection against self-incrimination and double jeopardy
6th	Rights to a speedy trial by jury, to hear accusations and confront the accuser, to witnesses, and to counsel
7th	Right to trial by jury in civil cases
8th	Protection against cruel and unusual punishment
9th	Protects rights not enumerated in the Constitution
10th	Limits the powers of the federal government to those designated in the Constitution

Additional Amendments	
11th	Sovereign immunity
12th	Revision of presidential election procedures
13th	Abolition of slavery
14th	Former slaves granted citizenship; equal protection; due process
15th	Citizens cannot be denied the right to vote based on race, color, or previous condition of servitude
16th	Income tax
17th	Direct election of U.S. Senators
18th	Prohibition of alcohol
19th	Women granted the right to vote
20th	Revision of inauguration date for presidents and vice-presidents
21st	Repeal of the 18th Amendment
22nd	Two-term limit for the presidency
23rd	District of Columbia granted representation in the electoral college
24th	Outlaws the poll tax
25th	Order of succession to the presidency; deals with the situation of presidential disability
26th	Lowers voting age to 18 (from 21)
27th	Delays laws about congressional salaries from going into effect until after the next congressional election

Key Documents and Speeches in U.S. History

While the Constitution is the most important document in the governance of the United States as it establishes the structures and processes of the governmental system, there are other documents that have played an important role in the nation as well. Throughout the history of the United States, there have been important documents and speeches that have shaped political life in this nation.

Document/Speech	**Written/Delivered By**	**When**	**Description**
Mayflower Compact	Pilgrims on the Mayflower	1620	Set up a temporary government for the Pilgrims at Plymouth Colony
Common Sense	Thomas Paine	1775	Pamphlet written to convince people to support the American Revolution
Declaration of Independence	Second Continental Congress; main author- Thomas Jefferson	1776	Stated reasons for the American Revolution and asserted the nation's independence from Great Britain
Articles of Confederation	Second Continental Congress	1781	Set up the first government for the newly independent United States
Federalist Papers	James Madison, Alexander Hamilton, John Jay	1787	Papers written to convince people to ratify the Constitution
U.S. Constitution	Constitutional Convention	1787	Document that set up the current system of U.S. government
Farewell Address	George Washington	1796	Departing President Washington advised the young nation against political factions and entangling foreign alliances
Gettysburg Address	Abraham Lincoln	1863	Speech given by President Lincoln in the midst of the Civil War as a memorial to those who died at the Battle of Gettysburg and to motivate the North to keep fighting to preserve the Union and to end slavery
Emancipation Proclamation	Abraham Lincoln	1865	Declared an end to slavery in the Confederate states

The Government of Massachusetts

Self-government and democracy in Massachusetts date back to the colonial settlement of the area by the Puritans. This group, used to a congregational style of church decision-making, applied this democratic principle to governance. One way in which many colonial Massachusetts communities employed self-government and democracy was through the use of the town meeting, which acted as a legislature in local affairs.

Many smaller communities in Massachusetts still uphold the tradition of the town meeting. In larger cities where this is not feasible, representative bodies are used instead. Local government exists at the county level as well, where elected representatives create legislation affecting the counties on matters that are not specific to and not under the jurisdiction of city or town governments.

At the state level, the executive is the governor. There is a bicameral legislature called the General Court, which consists of a Senate and a House of Representatives. Judicial power for the state resides in the Supreme Judicial Court.

Principles of Democracy and Citizenship

A democratic system relies on having citizens who are active participants. Citizens have certain rights and responsibilities to their nation.

In a democracy, the power of the government is limited and the leaders are ultimately responsible to the people. Citizens of the United States aged eighteen and older have the right to vote, which enables them to choose leaders who will represent their interests in the government. Citizens have a responsibility to stay knowledgeable about political issues and to vote according to their conscience to choose the best leaders for the nation.

Citizens can also practice good citizenship by staying politically active, well-informed, and involved in community service and activities. Responsible citizens understand that it takes a group of people working together for a community to function effectively.

Economics is a social science concerned with how goods and services are produced, bought, and sold. Students should understand fundamental economic principles, basic components of economic systems, and the relationship between economics and society.

There are two major division of economics—macroeconomics and microeconomics. **Macroeconomics** is the study of how economics works on a large scale, such as in a whole nation. **Microeconomics** is the study of economics on a smaller scale, looking at the decisions and impacts of individuals, small groups, and specific markets.

Resources are limited (**scarcity**), so people must make choices about how those resources will be allocated. On a small scale, individuals make choices about what they will buy and sell. On a larger scale, societies create economic systems that determine how goods will be produced, bought, and sold and by whom.

Economic Systems

Capitalism is a system in which property and the means of production are privately owned. What is produced, how much, and at what price is dictated by the market forces of **supply and demand**. If demand for a product is high, the supply will run low and prices will increase. If demand is low, the supply will be high and prices will decrease. The **profit motive** encourages hard work and innovation. Capitalism is also called a **market economy**. The purest form of capitalism is **laissez-faire**, in which the government takes a completely hands-off approach to the economic sector and allows market forces to regulate themselves.

Socialism is a system in which property is controlled collectively rather than individually. The purest form of socialism is **communism**, in which everything is owned in common and there is no private property and no social classes. In theory, communism eventually replaces the need for a government. In reality, however, nations that practice forms of communism tend to have very strong governments that take complete economic control. An economy in which the government has total control of the economy through centralized planning is called a **command** or a **planned economy**.

A **mixed economy** is a blend of capitalist and socialist principles, with both publicly and privately owned business operating at the same time.

A **closed economy** is one that is self-sufficient and cut off from outside influences, while an **open economy** allows for trade with other nations.

A **subsistence economy** is one in which people only produce that which is needed to survive.

The Role of the Government in the Economy

Different nations use different economic systems and therefore have different levels of governmental involvement in the economic sectors. A command economy gives the government complete control over economic decision-making, while a laissez-faire system allows the government no role and leaves economic decisions up to individuals and market forces. Most nations' systems are somewhere in the middle of these two extremes.

The United States is primarily a market economy but it does allow the government a degree of regulatory control. The government attempts to intervene in ways that will create a healthy, growing economic environment. Government involvement includes taxation, setting interest rates, regulating the monetary supply, regulating trade, and providing oversight.

Key Terms

Other important terms in the study of economics include:

- **Balance of trade**- a measure of a nation's exports vs. imports
- **Budget**- planning how current money will be allocated
- **Capital**- resources available for use; may be financial (money), natural, or human (labor)
- **Consumption**- the use of resources
- **Deflation-** an overall decrease in the price of goods and services
- **Depression**- a long period of economic decline, usually marked by inflation, high unemployment, and industrial decline
- **Exports-** goods sold to another country
- **Imports-** goods bought from another country
- **Inflation-** an overall increase in the price of goods and services

- **Profit-** the difference between revenue and cost
- **Recession-** a period of slow economic growth
- **Shortage-** when demand exceeds supply
- **Surplus**- when supply exceeds demand

World History

At the elementary level, studies of world history are focused on those events and cultures that have most shaped our modern world. They study the lasting contributions of classical civilizations as well as recent events that have most directly contributed to the current state of modern society. Students also learn to compare and contrast as they study world cultures.

Topics Addressed:

1. Early Human Societies
2. Classical Civilization
3. The Middle Ages
4. The Dawn of the Modern Era
5. The Twentieth Century and Beyond

Prehistoric Societies

The earliest humans were nomadic hunter-gatherers who migrated following their food sources.

All of this changed with the Neolithic Revolution. During the Neolithic Revolution, people learned how to farm and domesticate animals. This provided them with a steady, non-mobile food source, which enabled them to establish permanent settlements. These settlements eventually grew into cities and whole civilizations.

River Valley Civilizations

The earliest civilizations grew up in river valleys, due to the presence of fertile soil and water available for drinking, fishing, transportation, and trade. These early civilizations laid the foundations for later societies.

Civilization	Location	Major Contributions
Mesopotamian societies (e.g. Sumer, Babylon)	Tigris and Euphrates River Valley; modern-day Iraq	• Earliest form of writing (cuneiform) • First written law code (Code of Hammurabi) • Organization into city-states • Astronomy
Egypt	Nile River Valley	• Writing system (hieroglyphics) • Paper (papyrus) • Architecture (pyramids) • Strong government, military, and monetary system • Advancements in math
Huang He (Yellow River) Valley Civilizations	China	• Civil service • Advancements in math and science
Indus Valley Civilizations	India	• Built major cities • Advancements in math and science

Classical Civilizations

After the river valley civilizations paved the way for the creation of stable societies, classical civilizations emerged that were larger and stronger than their predecessors, and they would have an enormous lasting impact on future societies. These civilizations created strong governments, expanded trade, created militaries, expanded their territories, and created unified elements of culture, including religion.

Civilization	Major Characteristics and Contributions
China	• Dynastic cycle – leaders had mandate of heaven • Elaborate bureaucracy • Religions/philosophies- Daoism and Confucianism • Advancements in math, science, and technology
Greece	• Organized into city-states • Most city-states were oligarchies but Athens was a direct democracy • Polytheistic religion • High cultural period in the arts, philosophy, and architecture
Macedonia	• Created by Alexander the Great and fell apart soon after his death • Vast empire resulted in cultural diffusion between Greek and other cultures, resulting in a new blended culture called Hellenism
Rome	• Two major governmental periods- Republic and Empire • Unified law code- Twelve Tables • Extensive trade network • Advanced military • Engineering- aqueducts, road system • Polytheistic religion originally; later adopted Christianity • Important Leaders: Julius Caesar, Augustus, Constantine
Byzantine	• Formerly the Eastern Roman Empire that broke away from Rome • Practiced Orthodox Christianity • Important leader: Justinian, who created the Justinian Code
India	• Caste system (rigid social class structure) • Math- concept of zero, decimal system, Arabic numerals • Religions- Hinduism and Buddhism • Advancements in medicine, including the invention of plastic surgery
Mesoamerican Societies	• Major groups include the Mayas and Aztecs of Central American and the Incas of Peru • Aztecs had a strong centralized government and military • Mayas made great advancements in math and science • Incas (located in the Andes Mountains) created extensive road networks and used terrace farming

The Middle Ages are generally classified as the period from roughly 500-1400 C.E. This was the period between the fall of the Roman Empire, which had long dominated the world stage, until the reemergence of European strength in the Renaissance.

Medieval Europe

After the fall of the Roman Empire in 476 C.E., Europe lacked a strong central government and fell into a period of decentralization known as the Middle Ages or Medieval Period, which lasted from approximately 500-1400 C.E. During the Middle Ages, smaller governments were established under feudal systems.

In a feudal system, power is decentralized as rulers exchange vast plots land for oaths of loyalty. Great lords came to oversee large areas of land. Many of them would, in turn, offer pieces of land to lesser lords (known as vassals) in exchange for their loyalty to the lord. There was also a noble military class known as knights who also swore loyalty to local lords and/or to the king and whose duty it was to provide protection. A lord's estate was known as a manor, and the land was worked by a class of peasants known as serfs who were allowed to live on and farm the land in exchange for their loyalty and for providing crops for the lord's household. Serfs were legally bound to the manor and could not leave the manor lands without the permission of their lord.

These feudal governments lacked the power of Europe's former empires. In this vacuum of power, the Roman Catholic Church became the dominant authority in Europe and provided structure, organization, and unity.

Feudal Japan

For centuries, Japan also operated under a feudal system similar to that of Europe. In the Japanese class system, knights were known as samurai and the feudal lords as daimyo. A major difference from Europe was the distribution of power at the head of the kingdom, however. Whereas European kingdoms were led by a single monarch, the Japanese had two leaders. The emperor was considered divine and held in the highest regard, but was more of a ceremonial head of state with little practical power. The real authority was vested in the military ruler called the shogun. Dynasties during this time period were therefore known as shogunates.

The feudal system remained in Japan longer than it did in Europe. The last shogunate was the Tokugawa Shogunate, which ruled from 1600-1868.

Islamic Kingdoms

Islam was founded by Muhammad in what is now Saudi Arabia around 610. The religion quickly spread throughout the Middle East and rulers known as caliphs became both political and religious leaders of various kingdoms. Some of these kingdoms included the Umayyad Caliphate, the Abbasid Caliphate, the Ayyubid Dynasty, the Seljuks, the Ottoman Empire, and the Mughal Empire (Muslim kingdom in India). The most lasting and powerful of these kingdoms was the Ottoman Empire, which lasted from 1299-1923. One of its most significant rulers was Suleiman the Magnificent. Another famous ruler from this era is Saladin, founder of the Ayyubid Dynasty who presided over Jerusalem during the Crusades.

While Europe was experiencing the Dark Ages, Islamic kingdoms enjoyed a golden age, wherein the arts, literature, architecture, math, science, and medical knowledge thrived.

African Kingdoms

There were many powerful kingdoms in Africa prior to its colonization by the Europeans. These included the Mali, Ghana, Songhai, Axum, and Kush kingdoms. These kingdoms were able to prosper due to extensive trade, including the gold-salt trade.

The Renaissance and Reformation

Beginning in the mid-1400s, Europe underwent a gradual but significant change. Stronger kingdoms grew; there was a revival in arts, culture, and education; and commercial practices dramatically changed and brought great wealth to what became the major European powers. This period was known as the Renaissance or "rebirth."

The Renaissance began in Italy, whose strategic location on the Mediterranean made it ideal for trade. The subsequent influx of wealth allowed for patronage of the arts, while an influx of new ideas from other cultures contributed to the cultural shift and acquisition of new learning. Wealthy patrons such as the Medici family of Florence and political leaders such as Queen Elizabeth I of England supported this revival of learning and the arts.

During this same period, the Roman Catholic Church began to decline in power and some people began to question it. Martin Luther is credited with beginning the Protestant Reformation, in which people protested and broke away from the Catholic Church, in large part due to the church's corruption. The spread of these ideas was aided by a new invention, the printing press.

Absolutism, Enlightenment and Revolution

Governments continued to gain strength and many monarchs in Europe practiced absolutism, in which a ruler has total authority over the nation. This was based on a theory of divine right rule, in which people believed that the monarch's right to rule was granted by God so the ruler's authority came directly from God, giving the ruler much more power. The most famous example of an absolute monarch is Louis XIV of France, who called himself the "Sun King" and built an elaborate palace at Versailles.

In the late 17th and 18th centuries, there was a cultural movement which challenged these political traditions, as well as religious and other societal norms. This movement was known as the Enlightenment. Enlightenment thinkers began to speak and write about ways to improve society by focusing on rational thought, protecting human rights, and limiting government. Major Enlightenment philosophers include John Locke, Jean-Jacques Rousseau, and Voltaire.

Inspired by the democratic ideals of the Enlightenment, people eventually began to fight back against absolutism and several nations experienced revolutions. The largest of these was the French Revolution, which lasted from 1789-1799. Following the French Revolution, Napoleon Bonaparte rose to power in France and soon expanded French territory across much of Western Europe. Other nations across Europe experienced revolutions throughout the 19th century.

Industrialization and Imperialism

In the 18th and 19th centuries, the Industrial Revolution forever changed the world economy. Prior to the Industrial Revolution, goods were largely produced in people's homes or small shops and were made by hand. The Industrial Revolution brought about mechanization and the factory system, which allowed goods to be mass produced at a lower cost. This made goods cheaper and more widely available to the general population and served to create mass culture.

Industrialization had many effects on society. Populations became much more urbanized as people moved into the cities for factory jobs. Urban living and working conditions were poor, however, and social reforms eventually had to be made.

With the economic success that industrialization brought to many nations, several of those nations, especially those in Western Europe, began to look outside their own borders for sources of raw materials and new markets. This began a period (in the late 1800s to early 1900s) of widespread imperialism, wherein strong nations took control over weaker ones for their own gain. Much of Africa and Asia was colonized this way during this period.

World War I

World War I (1914-1918) was the first truly global war. It involved nations on every continent (except Antarctica) and changed the nature of modern warfare. The long-term causes of World War I can be summarized in the acronym MAIN—militarism, alliances, imperialism, and nationalism.

- **Militarism**- Nations were building up their military personnel and weapons, both as a precautionary measure and as a sign of national prestige.
- **Alliances**- Nations began to form competing alliances. Two major alliances formed in Europe—the Tripe Alliance (Germany, Austria-Hungary, and Italy) and the Triple Entente (Great Britain, France, and Russia).
- **Imperialism**- Nations were competing for economic and political control of overseas territories.
- **Nationalism**- National pride was high as nations competed. Nationalist movements within nations also contributed to unrest. For example, several ethnic groups wanted independence from Austria-Hungary.

The immediate cause of World War I was the assassination of Austro-Hungarian Archduke Franz Ferdinand by a Serbian nationalist in 1914. As Austria-Hungary debated retaliation, several nations joined each side of the struggle, viewing it as an opportunity to advance their own interests, and war quickly broke out. The two sides in the war were the Allied Powers and the Central Powers.

Major Combatants in World War I

Allied Powers	Central Powers
Great Britain France Russia (until 1917) Italy (after 1915) United States (after 1917)	Austria-Hungary Germany Ottoman Empire Bulgaria

World War I included new technology and combat methods that included machine guns, airplanes, tanks, trench warfare, and submarines.

The Allied Powers won the war, which officially ended with the **Treaty of Versailles**. The treaty heavily punished Germany for its role in the war, forcing it to demilitarize and pay reparations. The **League of Nations** was established as an international peacekeeping organization but was largely ineffective, due to its inability to enforce its policies and the failure of the United States to join.

The Interwar Period

Between World War I and World War II, major events included:

- **Russian Revolution** (1917-1921)- overthrow of the Russian czar and establishment of a communist state called the Soviet Union
- **Nationalist movements** in Turkey, Iran, and Saudi Arabia
- **Spanish Civil War** (1936-1939)
- **Great Depression**- worldwide economic collapse of the 1930s
- Rise of **totalitarian** regimes in Germany (Adolf Hitler), Italy (Benito Mussolini), Spain (Francisco Franco), and the Soviet Union (Joseph Stalin)

World War II

In the 1930s, totalitarian regimes such as Germany, Italy, and the Soviet Union began to try to expand their influence outward and take over other territories. Germany invaded Czechoslovakia, Italy invaded Ethiopia, and the Soviet Union spread into Eastern Europe. Japan, too, sought territorial expansion and invaded China.

During this period, Germany, under the leadership of Hitler and the Nazi regime, perpetrated the **Holocaust**, which resulted in the death of over six million Jews and others the Nazis thought of as undesirable, including the Roma (also known as gypsies,) homosexuals, the disabled, and the mentally ill. At first, other European nations such as Britain and France practiced **appeasement**, not wanting to enter another war. This failed, however, and when Hitler invaded Poland in 1939, war broke out and many other nations joined.

Major Combatants in World War II

Allied Powers	Axis Powers
Great Britain France Soviet Union United States (after 1941)	Germany Italy Japan

World War II lasted from 1939 until 1945, when the United States dropped atomic bombs on Japan. The agreement that ended the war was the Treaty of Paris. The United Nations was established as an international peacekeeping organization to replace the earlier, ineffective League of Nations.

The Postwar World

Following World War II, some of the major events of the twentieth and early twenty-first centuries included:

- The Cold War- a decades-long rivalry between the United States and the Soviet Union
- Communist Revolution in China (1949)
- Independence movements around the world, including India (led by Mahatma Gandhi) and many in Africa and the Middle East
- Ongoing Arab-Israeli conflict
- Nuclear proliferation – the worldwide spread of nuclear weapons
- Technological revolutions, including television, automobiles, computers, and the internet

Geography

Geography is the study of the physical features of the Earth. This includes both the natural landscape and the ways that humans interact with it.

Topics Addressed:

1. Elements of Geography
2. The World in Spatial Terms
3. Places and Regions
4. Physical Systems
5. Human Systems
6. Environment and Society
7. Uses of Geography

Elements of Geography

The study of geography is organized into six essential elements:

1. The World in Spatial Terms

- The geographic organization of the world

2. Places and Regions

- Place refers to an area whose boundaries are manmade, as well the physical and human characteristics of the location.
- Regions are geographic areas with unifying physical and/or human characteristics.

3. Physical Systems

- The natural landscape and processes of the Earth

4. Human Systems

- Processes and man-made societal structures by which humans organized themselves

5. Environment and Society

- The way that humans relate to their geographic surroundings

6. Uses of Geography

- How to study geography and the ways in which geographic knowledge can be utilized

The World in Spatial Terms

Spatial categories are used to divide the world into parts with common characteristics in order to better understand it.

The Earth is divided in halves called **hemispheres**. The Northern and Southern Hemispheres are divided by a line of latitude called the **equator**. The Eastern and Western Hemispheres are divided by a line of longitude called the **prime meridian**.

The largest masses on Earth are its seven **continents**—North America, South America, Europe, Asia, Africa, Australia, and Antarctica.

The largest bodies of water are called **oceans**. The world's oceans are the Atlantic, the Pacific, the Indian, the Arctic, and the Southern Oceans.

Specific places on Earth are identified as locations. A **location** is where a place is in the world, physically. Location can be absolute or relative.

- **Absolute location**- precise location on a map, given by coordinates (e.g. New York City is located at 40.7127° N, 74.0059° W.)
- **Relative location- the location of a place with respect to other places (e.g. New York City** is northwest of Philadelphia.)

Places and Regions

Places are areas whose boundaries are man-made. These include countries, states, territories, counties, cities, towns, etc.

Regions are areas that have common characteristics, both in the physical makeup of the land and in the culture of the people who live there. On the worldwide stage, some commonly identified regions include Latin America, the Middle East, and Southeast Asia.

Regions of the United States

Within the United States, the major regions are the West, the Southwest, the Midwest, the South, the Mid-Atlantic, and New England.

- The West includes the Pacific coastal area, which results in a temperate, wet climate. Running through this region are the Rocky Mountains, the largest mountain range in North America.
- The Southwest has a more hot, dry climate. Culturally, it is heavily influenced by the neighboring nation of Mexico.
- The Midwest contains America's Great Plains, which conduct a large share of the nation's agricultural production. The Mississippi River flows through the eastern portion of the region and the Great Lakes and Canada border it in the north.
- The South has a warmer, more humid climate, as much of it borders the Atlantic Ocean and the Gulf of Mexico. The Appalachian Mountains run along the eastern portion and the Mississippi Delta is located in Louisiana.
- The Mid-Atlantic region borders the Atlantic Ocean and the Great Lakes. It is home to mountains including the Adirondacks and the Catskills.
- New England is located along the rocky northeastern Atlantic coast of the United States.

Regions of Massachusetts

Massachusetts is a New England state whose capital and largest city is Boston. Massachusetts has several major regions:

- In the southeastern coastal region are lowlands and islands, including Martha's Vineyard and Nantucket. Just north of these islands is a peninsula containing Cape Cod, on the coast of Cape Cod Bay.
- In the central eastern coast is the Boston metropolitan area, which is densely populated. The city of Boston is located on Massachusetts Bay, at the mouth of the Charles River.
- The topography of central Massachusetts consists largely of rocky hills. It also contains much of the state's forest and farming areas.
- To the west of this is the Connecticut River Valley. The Connecticut River is Massachusetts' largest river. The river valley contains the state's richest soil.
- At the furthest western side of the state is a region known as the Berkshires, which contains the Berkshire Mountains as well as small portions of other ranges that spill over from other states.

Physical Systems

Physical systems are the component of geography concerned with the natural landscape and processes of the Earth.

Geographic Terms

Students will need to know important geographic terms used to describe the Earth's characteristics.

Term	Definition	Example in the U.S.	Example Outside the U.S.
Archipelago	Chain of islands	Hawaii	Japan
Bay	A body of water that is an inlet to a larger body of water such as an ocean or a sea	San Francisco Bay	Bay of Bengal
Canal	A man-made waterway	Erie Canal	Panama Canal
Channel	A narrow body of water that connects two other bodies of water	Houston Ship Channel	English Channel
Delta	Low, wet, triangular piece of land at the mouth of a river	Mississippi Delta	Nile Delta
Desert	Area with little to no precipitation	Desert	Sahara Desert
Gulf	A large body of water partially enclosed by land that connects to an ocean or sea	Gulf of Mexico	Persian Gulf
Island	A piece of land surrounded on all sides by water	Puerto Rico	Cuba
Isthmus	A very narrow strip of land connecting two larger pieces of land with water on both sides	Madison Isthmus	Isthmus of Panama
Lake	A body of water completely surrounded by land	Lake Ontario	Lake Titicaca
Mountain	A very high rocky formation	Rocky Mountains	Andes Mountains

Term	Definition	Example in the U.S.	Example Outside the U.S.
Peninsula	A piece of land with water on three sides	Florida	India
Plains	Flat, grassy lands	The Great Plains	The Great Steppe
River	A long, flowing body of water that empties into a larger body of water	The Mississippi River	The Amazon River
Sea	A large saltwater body, smaller than an ocean	Bering Sea	Mediterranean Sea
Valley	Low area between mountains	Death Valley	Danube Valley

Climates and Biomes

Climates are long-term weather patterns for a particular area. The primary climates on Earth are:

- **Tropical**- hot and wet year-round
- **Dry**- temperature varies widely from day to night; very little precipitation
- **Temperate**- warm and wet in the summer, cool and dry in the winter
- **Continental**- found on large land masses, this climate has fairly low precipitation and temperatures can vary widely
- **Polar**- very cold; permanently frozen ground

Biomes are large areas that have distinct sets of plant and animal life that are well-adapted to the environment. Biomes are classified according to geography and climate. The major biomes are:

- **Alpine**- mountain regions that are cold and snowy
- **Chaparra**l- hot and dry; landscape varies- could contain plains, hills, and/or mountains
- **Deciduous forest-** contains many trees; four distinct seasons (spring, summer, fall, winter)
- **Desert-** flat land with very little precipitation
- **Grasslands-** interior flatlands with lots of grass and other low plant life; tropical or temperate climate
- **Rainforest-** tropical climate; dense vegetation
- **Savanna-** grasslands with warm temperatures year-round with a dry and a rainy season
- **Taiga-** cold, snowy winters and warm, humid summers
- **Tundra-** very cold; little vegetation; polar climate

Human Systems

Humans systems are processes and man-made societal structures by which humans organized themselves.

The Organization of Human Societies

Throughout history, humans have organized themselves into societies for their mutual benefit. Societal living offers protection and the ability to pool resources. In order to maintain order in societies, people tend to organize in certain ways. Societal structures range from the very simple to the complex.

- **Family**- The most basic organizational structure of societies is the family unit. Family structures and relationships vary across cultures. Some societies are patriarchal (led by the eldest male) while others are matriarchal (led by the eldest female). Some cultures value filial piety (respect for elders) more than others. Culture also dictates traditions for marriage and raising children.

- **Neighborhoods and Communities**- Groups of families living together in close proximity create neighborhoods and communities. Culture impacts the way that communities cooperate or compete. Some cultures place a high value on self-sufficiency, while others see more merit in interdependence.

- **Formal political structures**- Some structures of society are formal and political in nature. Geographical boundaries and governments dictate who is part of a group. These organizational structures range from villages and towns at the local level up to very large scale organizations like nations and empires.

- **Informal cultural structures**- People can belong to more informal organizations as well. This can include ethnic or cultural groups, religions and religious organizations, and other socially-based groups.

Population Growth

The world population is growing, but the rate of growth has varied greatly over time. Birth and death rates, which cause populations to grow or decline, are influenced by many factors, including:

- Supplies of food, water, and other resources
- Violence
- Disease
- Medical advancements
- Technology

Patterns of Migration

The movement of groups of people is called migration. Migration takes two major forms:

1. Immigration- movement into a new area or country
2. Emigration- movement out of an area or country

Migration is caused by many factors. Factors that cause people to emigrate from their homeland are called "push factors." Factors that draw people to immigrate to a new area are called "pull factors." Here are some common ones:

Push Factors	Pull Factors
Warfare	Peace
Disease	Health
Famine	Resources
Lack of opportunity	Economic opportunities such as jobs
Economic struggle	Opportunity for social mobility
Lack of social mobility	

Cultural Transmission

Throughout learning about social studies, students will encounter information about people groups, both past and present, with varied cultural backgrounds. Students should try to gain understanding of how peoples' cultural backgrounds are tied to their interactions with the world around them.

Cultures undergo change over time, and a major reason for this is that cultures frequently come into contact with one another and ideas are shared. This is called the **transmission of culture** or **cultural diffusion**.

Culture is transmitted by many means, including:

- Trade and commerce
- Travel/exploration
- Warfare and conquest
- Missionary activities
- International cooperation
- Communication via technology

Human Effects on the Environment

Humans, more than any other creatures, have the capacity to alter their environments. Human settlements have an enormous impact on the physical systems of the Earth. One major way that humans affect the natural environment is through construction. Building transportation systems, buildings, and other structures alters the landscape and displaces the organisms that once inhabited that space.

Another way humans affect the environment is by using natural resources. Earth has a limited amount of natural resources and growing human populations and advanced technology have increased the demand for those resources over time, putting a strain on the natural environment. Along with construction and the use of natural resources also comes pollution. Human activity creates waste byproducts that can be harmful to the environment.

Environmental Effects on Humans

Likewise, physical systems affects humans and they must learn to adapt to environmental factors. Physical features influence where humans will settle, what kind of communities and industries they can build there, and how easily those communities will be able to connect with other communities. For example, because of the difficult terrain, fewer people live in mountainous regions than in lowlands. Those societies that do live in the mountains have made adaptations such as terrace farming in order to survive in that environment. These communities have historically also found themselves isolated from the outside world due to the natural barriers that the mountains create. Geography also affects day to day life in ways such as the foods that people eat, the clothing they wear, and the type of housing they live in.

Uses of Geography

The study of geography has many uses. It helps to make sense of the world and to picture the physical relationships between people, groups and environments. Historically, it helps people understand why societies have settled where they have and why they developed in the ways that they did. It helps to understand the causes of conflicts between both historical and contemporary groups. It can also help to plan for the future by allowing for the examination of the distribution of people and resources throughout the world.

Using Visual Tools

There are many visual tools that can aid students in understanding Social Science content. These include maps, charts, political cartoons, photographs, illustrations, multimedia sources, and more. Students should analyze these sources carefully, checking for labels, captions, scales, and other details that can help them understand the information in the source.

Maps

One particularly important skill in Social Studies is knowing how to read and create maps. A **map** is a visual representation of a physical space. There are many types of maps, including physical maps, political maps, topographic maps, thematic maps, climate maps, historical maps, and population maps. Some key features of maps that students should know are:

- **Lines of latitude and longitude**- lines marking the distance of a location from the equator (latitude) and the prime meridian (longitude)
- **Compass rose**- symbol on a map showing the cardinal directions
- **Legend/Key**- box on a map that shows what the symbols and/or colors on a map represent
- **Scale**- Shows how distances on the map compare to real-life distances

Science, Technology, and Engineering

Scientific knowledge is an essential part of students' academic foundation for life. Students develop skills in critical thinking, problem solving, and scientific methodology while learning about natural, physical, and chemical processes.

Test Structure

The Science, Technology, and Engineering section makes up 30% of the Multi-Subject subtest. Within this section, there are five major subcategories with which you must be familiar:

A. Life Science

B. Physical Science

C. Earth Science

D. The Foundations of Scientific Thought

E. Scientific Inquiry and Experimentation

Each subcategory is divided into topics, which state the skills you must be able to demonstrate on the exam.

Life Science

Life science is the study of living things on Earth, including their characteristics, biological processes, behaviors, history, and relationships.

Topics Addressed:

1. Characteristics of Living Things
2. Life Cycles, Reproduction, Heredity, and Evolution
3. Organisms and the Environment

In science anything that is or has ever been alive is considered a living thing. Anything that has never and never will be alive is considered a non-living thing.

Characteristics of Living Things

Living things share several common traits:

- Require nourishment
- Use energy
- Are capable of growth
- Reproduce
- Have definite life spans
- Respond and adapt to their environment
- Are made up of **cells**

Cells

Living things are made up of cells. The purposes of cells are to create energy for the organism, to create proteins, and to reproduce.

Cells are organized in the following manner:

- **Tissue**- a group of cells
- **Organ**- a group of tissues working together for a common purpose
- **Organ system**- a group of organs working together
- **Organism**- a complete living thing, made up of systems

Plant and Animal Cells

Plant cells and animal cells share many similarities but plant cells contain some parts that animal cells do not.

Parts of Plant and Animal Cells	
Part	**Function**
Nucleus	Control center of the cell which contains DNA
Cytoplasm	Everything outside the nucleus
Endoplasmic reticulum	Transport system for molecules between the nucleus and the cytoplasm
Ribosomes	Make proteins
Golgi bodies	Package and transport proteins
Mitochondria	Create energy (ATP)
Vacuoles	Store food and water
Lysosomes	The digestive system of the cell; holds enzymes that are used to break down molecules
Cell membrane	Permeable boundary of the cell that allows the passage of needed

Parts Only Found in Plant Cells	
Chloroplasts	Contain chlorophyll, used in food production (photosynthesis)
Cell wall	Rigid outer structure of the cell materials in and waste out
Cell membrane	Permeable boundary of the cell that allows the passage of needed

Animal cell:

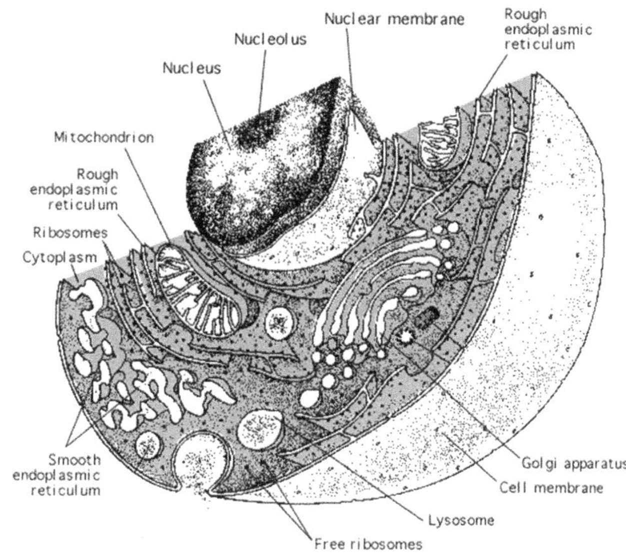

Plant cell:

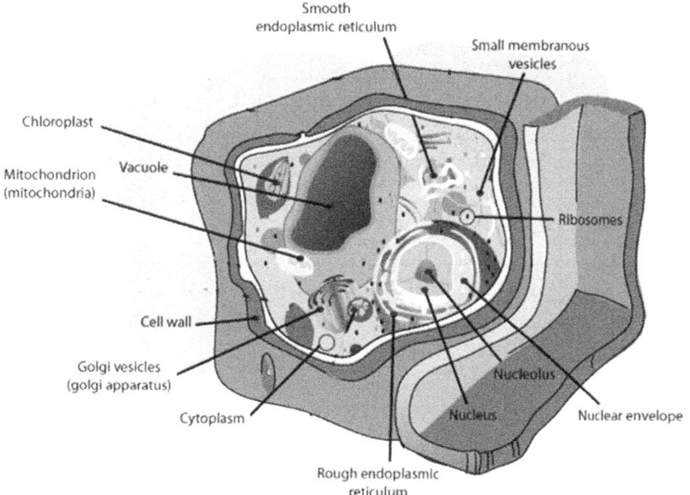

Structure of Plants

Part	Function
Roots	Hold the plant into the ground; absorb water and nutrients from the soil
Stem	Carry nutrients from the roots to the rest of the plant
Leaves	Make food for the plant through photosynthesis, a process by which the plant uses its chlorophyll, water, nutrients, carbon dioxide, and energy from the sun to make food and oxygen
Flower	Site of reproduction

Structure of Animals

Animals' organ systems provide the basic functions which enable them to live. While animals all possess some form of these systems, the organs they contain may differ among species. The chart below contains information about each system and provides the names of some of the human body parts for these systems.

System	Function
Digestive	Provides nutrition to the body
Circulatory	Carries blood throughout the body
Respiratory	Brings in oxygen and expels carbon dioxide
Excretory	Eliminates waste
Nervous	Carries electrical signals from brain to the cells
Reproductive	Creates offspring
Muscular and/or Skeletal	Provides structure and allows movement
Regulatory	Regulates body functions

Human Body Systems

The human body contains the following systems:

System	Function	Body Parts Involved
Digestive	Provides nutrition to the body	Mouth, tongue, esophagus, stomach, large and small intestines
Circulatory	Carries blood throughout the body	Heart, veins, arteries
Respiratory	Brings in oxygen and expels carbon dioxide	Nose, mouth, trachea, lungs
Excretory	Eliminates waste	Skin, kidneys, bladder
Nervous	Carries electrical signals from brain to the cells	Brain, nerves
Reproductive	Creates offspring	Uterus, ovaries, testes, penis
Muscular	Allows movement	Muscles
Skeletal	Provides structure and allows movement	Bones
Endocrine	Regulates body functions through hormones	Brain, glands throughout the body, pancreas
Immune	Defends the body from illness	T-cells carried by blood
Lymphatic	Removes excess fluid from around cells; eliminates bacteria	Lymph nodes
Integumentary	Protects the body against the environment	Skin, hair, nails

Life Cycles

One of the characteristics of a living thing is that it has a finite life span. Every organism goes through a life cycle, made up of the various stages that are common to all living things:

1. The organism comes into existence
2. Growth
3. Metamorphosis
4. Maturation
5. Reproduction
6. Death

Reproduction and Heredity

Reproduction is the creation of new organisms of the same species. Reproduction is essential for the continuation of the species. **DNA** (deoxyribonucleic acid) contains the codes for proteins, which are the building blocks of life. DNA is made up of two strands that contain **genes** that dictate traits for an organism. Groups of genes make up **chromosomes.**

Organisms reproduce using one of two types of reproduction:

1. **Asexual reproduction**- New cells are created from only one parent organism via cells that produce two identical sets of chromosomes and then split to form new cells.
2. **Sexual reproduction**- Reproduction involves two parent organisms, each of whom contribute a reproductive cell containing one set of chromosomes. The two combine to create cells with a full set of chromosomes.

Chromosomes come in pairs and each half of the pair comes with genes for each trait. The combination of these genes determine the organism's traits. Traits can be classified as either **dominant** or **recessive.**

Dominant genes are more likely to appear in an organism. Recessive genes will generally be hidden by dominant genes if dominant genes are also present.

If there are two dominant genes, the dominant trait will appear in the organism. If there is one dominant and one recessive gene, the dominant trait will appear in the organism. If both genes are recessive, the recessive trait will appear in the organism.

For example, brown eyes are a trait that is dominant over blue eyes. If each parent contributes genes for both brown (B) and blue (b) eyes, the possibilities for the child will be:

	B	**b**
B	BB	Bb
b	Bb	bb

If even one dominant trait (B) is present in a pair, it will appear in the organism, therefore, in three out of the four possible combinations of genes for this child (75%), the child will have brown eyes.

Biological Evolution

The way that species change over time is through biological evolution. Most of the times, offspring have genes like their parents. Occasionally, however, mistakes in the DNA duplication process result in abnormalities called mutations. Most mutations are benign and some are negative, but sometimes a mutation actually has a positive effect for the organism. A positive mutation may make it easier for the organism to survive and reproduce. When this happens, the process of natural selection makes it so that eventually, most of the members of that species will come to possess the favorable mutation.

Natural selection is the process by which those traits that are beneficial to organisms are produced and passed on in the species. Natural selection is based on a premise of the "survival of the fittest," which says that those organisms best genetically equipped to survive and reproduce will survive and will have their traits passed on. Those organisms that are weaker will eventually die off and with them, their less favorable traits.

Over time, the process of natural selection can result in significant changes to a species.

Organisms and the Environment

Organisms all share space on the Earth and must therefore live in cooperation in order to survive.

The **biosphere** is the environment on Earth in which living things exist. It includes the land, the water, and the air.

Within the biosphere are smaller environments, known as ecosystems. An **ecosystem** is a community of organisms and their physical environment. An ecosystem requires an energy source (such as the sun), a means to convert that energy to glucose (plant life), and a means of recycling organic materials.

Ecosystems operate and transfer energy according to a cycle:

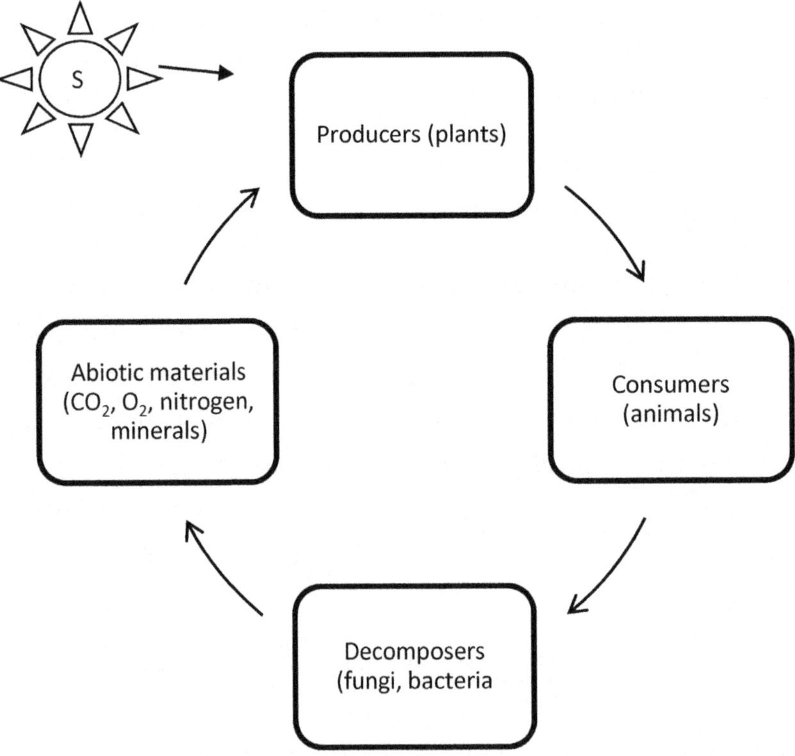

The Food Chain

The way that energy moves through living things in an ecosystem is through the **food chain**. The food chain describes the order in which animals consume plants and other animals.

Plants create energy in the form of ATP through photosynthesis. They are known as **producers**. To get this energy for themselves, animals must either eat those plants (herbivores) or eat another animal (carnivore), which somewhere down the line has eaten a plant and gotten its energy.

Animals are known as **consumers** because they consume (eat) other organisms. Those who eat plants are known as primary consumers. Those who eat primary consumers are known as secondary consumers, etc. At the highest level of a food chain are those top consumers who have few natural predators and are therefore unlikely to be eaten.

Here is an example of a food chain in an ecosystem:

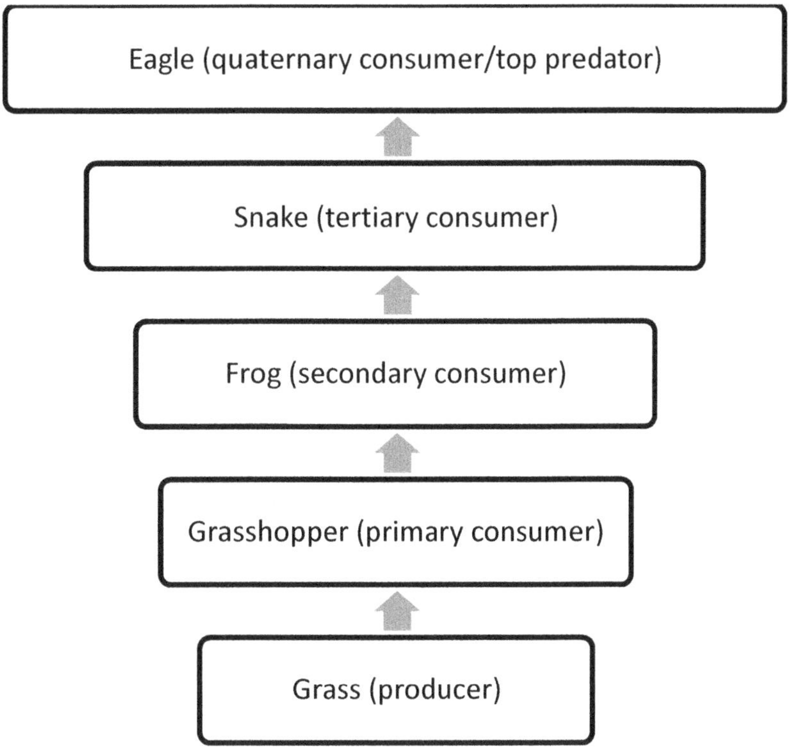

Disruptions to Ecosystems

The balance of ecosystems is delicate and can be disrupted by many causes that include:

- Interruptions in the food chain
- Depletion of any species
- Natural disasters
- Change in energy supply
- Human causes, such as pollution, deforestation, depletion of resources, mining, and radiation

Physical Science

Physical science is the study of the physical and chemical materials, processes, and forces that make up our environment.

Topics Addressed:

1. The Structure and Properties of Matter
2. Energy
3. Forces and Motion
4. Engineering Applications

The Atomic Structure of Matter

Matter is the physical substance of which everything is composed. Matter comes in many different varieties and can even change forms.

The most basic unit of matter is the **atom**. An atom is made up of a center cluster of positively charged **protons** and non-charged **neutrons** called a **nucleus**, as well as outer layers of negatively charged **electrons.**

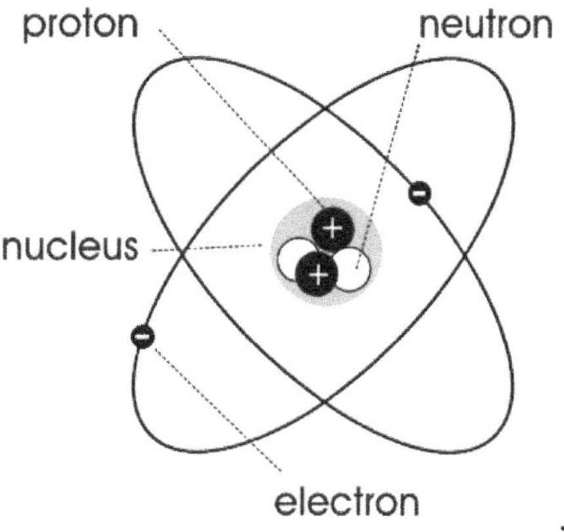

An **element** is a type of substance that cannot be broken down into different types of matter. Currently there are 114 known elements and they are listed by atomic number in the **periodic table**.

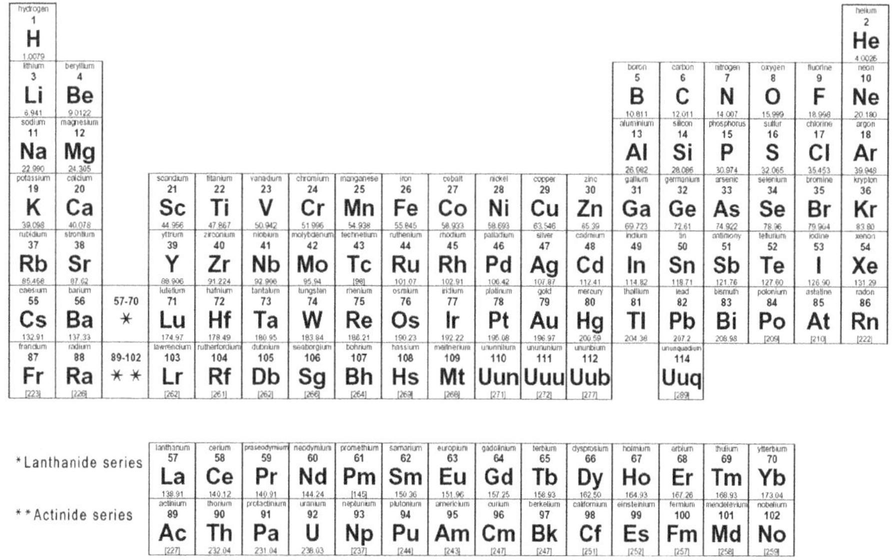

How Elements Combine

Elements combine in different ways to make up all matter. Two or more atoms combined into an electrically neutral structure are called a **molecule**. Molecules can contain atoms that are of the same element or of different elements.

A **compound** is the chemical bonding of two or more different elements.

Mixtures occur when two unlike substances are mixed together without a chemical reaction. Mixtures can be **homogeneous** (if they are the same throughout) or **heterogeneous** (if the components are not distributed uniformly).

Solutions occur when one type of substance (called the **solute**) dissolves into another substance (called the **solvent**). Solutions are considered homogenous mixtures because the new substance is the same throughout as the solute is distributed evenly.

States of Matter

Matter can exist in three forms or states—solid, liquid, and gas.

- **Solids** have molecules that are relatively close together and have strong molecular forces that hold the substance into a fixed shape with a fixed volume.
- **Liquids** have weaker molecular forces than solids, which allow them to move fluidly and take on the shape of their container, while still maintaining a fixed volume.
- **Gases** have weak molecular bonds which allow the molecules to move rapidly. Gases take on both the shape and volume of their containers, as they will spread out as far as their container will allow.

Matter can change its state through changes in temperature and pressure. These changes are called **phases changes**.

From	To	Name of Change
Solid	Liquid	Melting
Solid	Gas	Sublimation
Liquid	Gas	Vaporization
Liquid	Solid	Freezing
Gas	Liquid	Condensation
Gas	Solid	Deposition

Properties of Matter

Matter can be described according to certain properties. These include:

- Mass- a measure of the amount of matter in an object
- Volume- the amount of space an object or substance takes up
- Points of phase change- the temperature at which a certain substance undergoes a phase change (i.e. boiling point, freezing point)
- Hardness- a measure of how resistant a subject is to physical change (e.g., scratching, indentation) when force is applied
- Texture- the tactile quality of a surface

Matter is also subject to certain physical laws. The **Law of Conservation of Matter** states that matter can be neither created nor destroyed, but it can be rearranged.

Physical and Chemical Changes

Changes in matter can be classified as either physical or chemical.

Physical changes affect the form of a substance but not its chemical composition. Some examples of physical changes are:

- Phases changes (boiling, melting, freezing, etc.)
- Tearing
- Crumpling

Chemical changes do involve an alteration of the chemical composition of a substance at the molecular level. Some examples of chemical changes are:

- Burning
- Rusting
- Cooking

Energy is defined as the ability to do work. Energy comes in several different forms, including kinetic, potential, thermal, radiant, electrical, mechanical, chemical, and nuclear. While energy cannot be created or destroyed (**Law of Conservation of Energy**) it can be transferred to another form.

Kinetic and Potential Energy

The two most basic states of energy are kinetic and potential. **Kinetic energy** is energy in motion. **Potential energy** is stored energy that can be converted to kinetic energy. An object in motion has kinetic energy, while an object at rest has potential energy.

Thermal Energy

Thermal energy (or **heat**) is the energy of a substance or system related to its temperature. Heat is caused by the vibration of molecules. The faster the vibration, the more heat will be produced.

Heat can be transferred in three major ways:

1. **Conduction**- heat transfer via a conductive material such as metal
2. **Convection**- heat transfer through the collision of liquid or gas molecules
3. **Radiation**- heat is transmitted without contact via infrared radiation

Radiant Energy

Radiant energy is the energy of electromagnetic waves such as light.

Electric Energy

Electric energy is a form of energy that is delivered or absorbed by an electrical circuit. An **electrical circuit** is the path along which an electrical current flows. There are two main types of circuits:

- **Series circuit**- circuit in which resistors are arranged in a chain so that the current only has only path to take
- **Parallel circuit**- resistors are arranged so that there are multiple paths for the current to pass through

Conductors are those materials that allow electrical current to flow through them, such as metals. **Insulators** are those materials that do not allow the flow of electrical currents, such as plastic and wood.

Mechanical Energy

Mechanical energy is related to the use of machines.

Chemical Energy

Chemical energy is the energy stored in the bonds between atoms in molecules. Chemical energy contains the potential for a **chemical reaction**, wherein one set of chemical substances is transformed into another.

Nuclear Energy

Nuclear energy results from a change in the nucleus of atoms. There are two types of nuclear reactions. When nuclei are split, this is called **fission**. Fission is the type of reaction used in creating atomic bombs and nuclear reactors. The joining of nuclei is called **fusion**, which occurs in the sun and in hydrogen bombs.

Interactions Between Energy and Matter

Energy can interact with matter in a variety of ways. This includes:

- **Electricity** moves through matter (specifically, a conductor) as a current. Electricity can produce light, heat, motion, and magnetic force. Electricity can be measured in terms of voltage and amperage. **Voltage** is a measure of the amount of force in an electrical current. **Amperage** measures the strength of an electrical current as it passes through a conductor.

- **Magnetism** involves the forces exerted by magnets on other magnets. All magnets have two poles (called "North" and "South") which have opposite charges. Opposite poles attract one another, while similar poles repel.

- **Sound** moves in waves caused by the vibrations of particles. The three major characteristics of sound are pitch, amplitude, and quality. Differences in **pitch** are cause by the rate of the vibrations. The faster the vibrations, the higher the pitch. **Amplitude** is how loud a sound is, which is caused by the force used to create the sound. The greater the force that created the sound, the louder the sound will be. Sound **quality** is also known as timbre and includes other characteristics that allow the ear to distinguish between sounds of the same pitch and amplitude.

Forces and Motion

Motion

Motion is change is an object's position. The fundamental principles of motion are those found in Newton's Laws of Motion. His three laws are:

1. An object in motion will stay in motion and an object at rest will stay at rest until acted upon by an outside force. (inertia)
2. An object will move in the direction of the force that was applied to it, with an acceleration proportional to the force applied. Force = mass x acceleration
3. For every action, there is an equal and opposite reaction.

Force

Force is an influence that causes an object to undergo a change in motion. There are different types:

Type	Definition
Applied Force	Force applied directly to an object by another object or person (e.g. pushing and pulling)
Gravity	The force with which a massively large object (such as the Earth or another planet or moon) pulls other, smaller objects toward itself ; gravity on Earth pulls everything toward the Earth's center
Friction	The force exerted by an object or surface as another object slides across it
Air Resistance	Force exerted upon objects as they move through the air
Normal Force	The support force applied when an object comes is in contact with another stable object
Tension Force	Force present in a cable when pulled on both ends
Spring Force	The force a spring exerts on any object attached to it
Electromagnetic Force	A natural force that affects electrically charged particles

When the result of all forces acting on an object is zero, the object is said to be in equilibrium and is either at rest or is in unaccelerated motion.

Simple Machines

The most basic types of machines are known as simple machines. These systems perform work with very few parts.

There are six basic types of simple machines:

Simple Machine	Description	Example
Incline Plane	Used to help move things up or down by reducing the force needed by increasing the distance	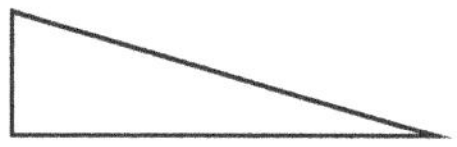
Lever	Used to lift a load using applied force and a fulcrum or pivot	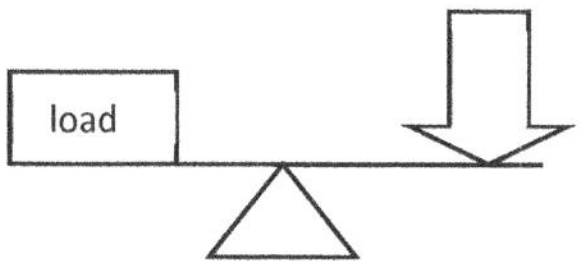 load
Pulley	A system that uses a wheel and a rope to make it easier to lift things	
Screw	An inclined plane wrapped around a pole that can be used for holding objects together or for lifting	
Wedge	An object with at least one slanting side resulting in a very narrow edge, used to separate or cut things	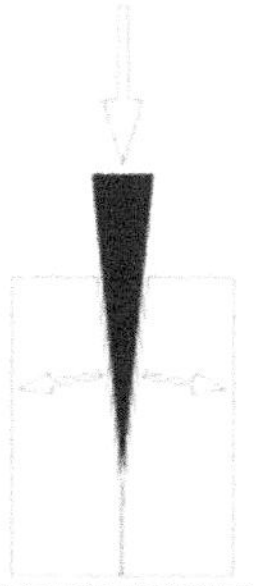
Wheel and Axle	Allows objects to move more quickly and easily by rolling them	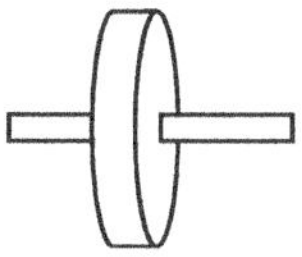

Engineering Applications

Physical science finds practical application in the field of engineering. Engineers apply their knowledge of science and mathematics to solve problems by designing materials, structures, and systems. In this way, they provide the link between science and its usefulness for addressing human needs on a practical level.

There are many different fields of engineering, all of which apply the physical sciences in different ways. Some of the major branches of engineering are:

- Chemical Engineering
- Civil Engineering
- Electrical Engineering
- Mechanical Engineering

Earth Science

Earth science is the study of the Earth, its composition, its history, its place in the universe, and its natural processes.

Topics Addressed:

1. The Structure and Processes of the Earth
2. Atmosphere, Climate, and Weather
3. The Earth in the Universe

The Structure of the Earth

Layers of the Earth

The Earth is composed of layers, each different in its composition.

- **Inner core**- the spherical solid center of the Earth, composed largely of iron and nickel; about 700-800 miles in diameter
- **Outer core**- a layer of liquid iron and nickel about 1,400 miles thick
- **Mantle**- a layer of hot, semi-solid rock about 1,800 miles thick that has currents, causing the plates of crust on top of it to move
- **Crust**- a series of solid plates that cover the Earth's surface, ranging from 5 to 30 miles thick

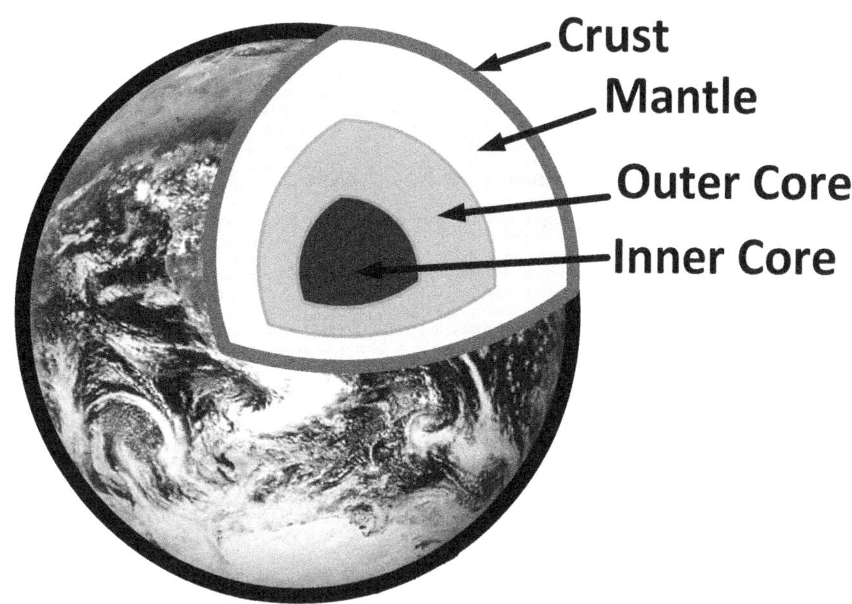

Plate Tectonics

The crust consists of continental (land) plates and oceanic plates. These plates are constantly shifted atop the mantle. The movement of these plates is known as **plate tectonics.**

The boundaries between plates help to shape the Earth's surface and can cause geological events. There are three ways plates can interact at their boundaries:

Type of Boundary	Example	Results
Convergent (colliding)	→ ←	Mountains, ridges, volcanoes
Divergent (separating)	← →	Bodies of water, new crust
Transform (rubbing)	↑ ↓	Earthquakes

The Earth's History

Geological history is the study of how Earth has developed over time. The Earth is estimated to be between 4 and 5 billion years old. Over the course of its history, the Earth's landforms and life forms have undergone a great deal of change.

The **geologic record** helps scientists to learn about different parts of the Earth's history by examining layers of rock. Scientists base their findings on the law of superposition, which says that the oldest rocks are found at the bottom and newer rocks are found at the top. This helps scientists to date events and create a timeline of Earth's history.

Paleontology is the study of fossils. These scientists can study the origins and history of life by looking at the fossils contained within the layers of rock that compose the Earth. The evolution of life is examined in greater detail in the Life Science section.

The Earth's history is divided into two major time periods called eons:

Precambrian Eon	Phanerozoic Eon		
From the beginning of the Earth to the formation of life	From the formation of life to the present day Divided into three eras:		
	Paleozoic Era	**Mesozoic Era**	**Cenozoic Era**
	Approx. 542-251 million years ago Rise of early life including trilobites, shellfish, corals, sponges, fish, land plants like ferns and trees, insects, amphibians, and reptiles	Approx. 251-65 million years ago Rise of dinosaurs, mammals, birds, and flowering plants Also later included the extinction of dinosaurs	Approx. 65 million years ago to present day Rise of primates, including hominids and eventually modern humans

The Processes of the Earth System

The Earth operates according to several systems and processes, all of which are interrelated and work together to create an environment in which life is sustainable.

The Earth's Position

The **tilt** of the Earth on its axis determines the amount of direct radiation from the sun at any given point on Earth. Locations closest to the equator receive the most direct solar rays and are therefore warmer throughout the year than the poles.

The **rotation** of the Earth is responsible for night and day and the gain and loss of heat and sunlight that accompany those times of day.

The **revolution** of the Earth around the sun is responsible for the changing of the seasons.

Heat

Heat is a process that greatly affects everything else on Earth. The Earth's heat comes from:

- Radioactivity at the Earth's core, which is responsible for the movement of plates and thus the creation of landforms.
- Solar energy, which heats Earth's surface.

Geological Processes

Geological processes are processes at work on the Earth's landforms. There are three major types of rocks, shown in the following chart:

Type of Rock	Description	Examples
Igneous	Formed through the cooling of magma	Granite, obsidian, pumice
Sedimentary	Formed when sediments (bits of eroded rock, sand, shells, fossils, etc.) are compressed into hard layers over time	Sandstone, limestone, shale
Metamorphic	Formerly igneous and sedimentary rocks that have morphed due to heat and pressure	Marble, quartzite, slate

These rock layers that make up the Earth's surface can change over time through forces such as weathering and erosion. **Weathering** is the breaking down of rock via environmental forces.

- Physical weathering occurs due to interaction with natural physical forces such as water, ice, and wind.
- Chemical weathering occurs due to exposure to chemicals, such as acid rain breaking down rock or oxygen in the air causing oxidation of a surface.

Erosion is when pieces of the weathered material are carried away via wind and water. Over time, these changes can have dramatic effects on the landscape, such as when a river erodes a plateau and forms a canyon.

One result of the breakdown of rock is the formation of soil. **Soil** is the loose material that sits on top of the rock on the Earth's surface. It is the substance in which many of Earth's plants grow. Its formation is the result of the physical and chemical breakdown of rock over time. In addition to rock, soil also contains dissolved minerals and organic material from decomposed plants and animals.

The **rock cycle** describes how rocks are created, changed, and destroyed.

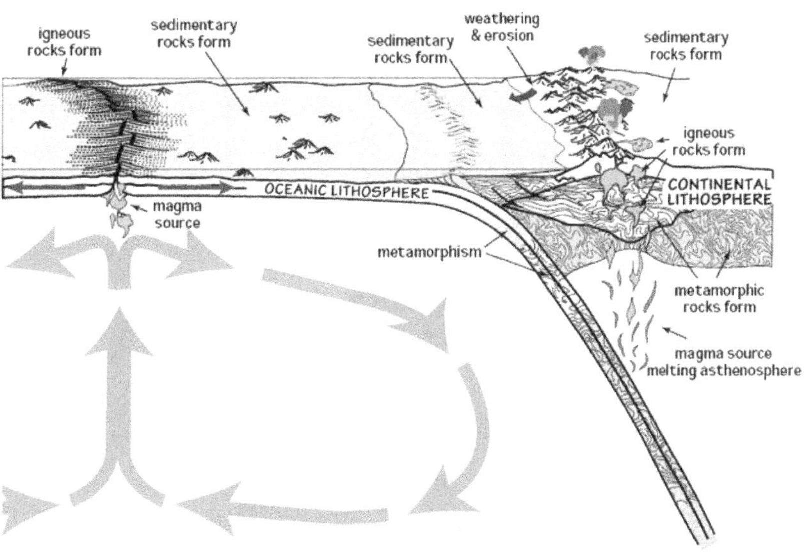

Water Cycle

The **water cycle** shows how water circulates through the Earth's surface and atmosphere.

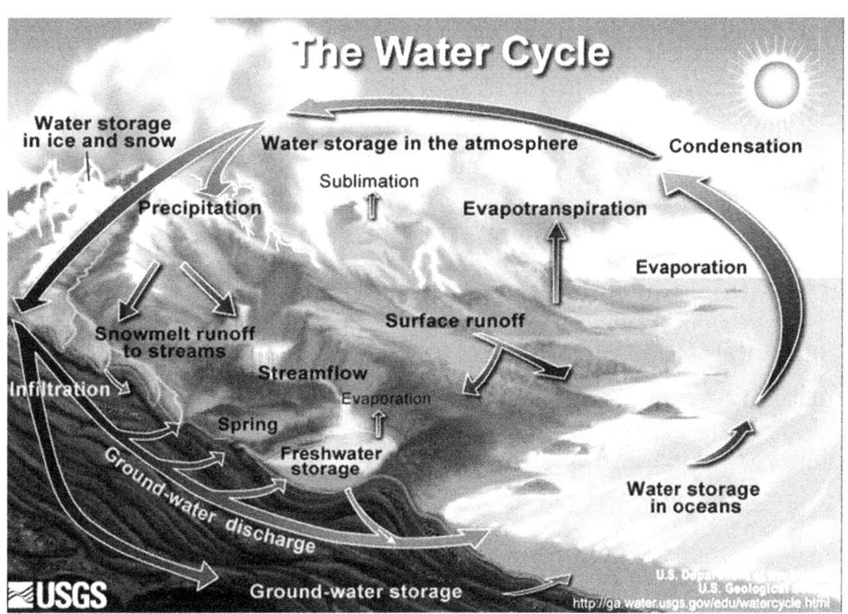

Layers of the Atmosphere

The atmosphere (the air above Earth) also exists in layers.

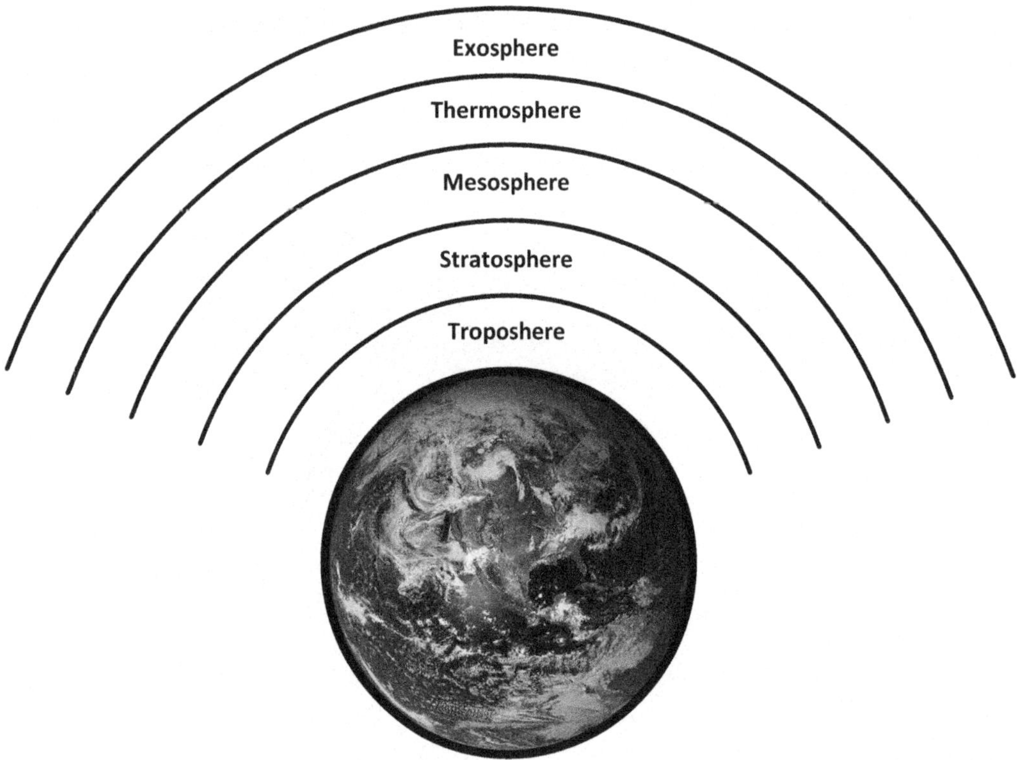

Climates

Climates are long-term weather patterns for a particular area. The primary climates on Earth are:

- Tropical- hot and wet year-round
- Dry- temperature varies widely from day to night; very little precipitation
- Temperate- warm and wet in the summer, cool and dry in the winter
- Continental- found on large land masses, this climate has fairly low precipitation and temperatures can vary widely
- Polar- very cold; permanently frozen ground

Weather

Weather is the state of the atmosphere at a particular time and place, including temperature, air movement, precipitation, and humidity. The water cycle plays an enormous role in the weather, as it creates precipitation.

Clouds are the source of precipitation, as they are formed from accumulated moisture in the air. There are several major types of clouds:

Cloud Type	Description
Stratus	Horizontal layered clouds formed when warm, moist air passes over cool air
Cumulus	Large, puffy white clouds formed when warm, moist air is forced upward
Cirrus	Wispy clouds containing ice crystals that form at high altitudes
Nimbus	Clouds that produce precipitation

Air masses are large bodies of air that are fairly uniform as far as temperature, pressure, and moisture levels. Air masses have a significant impact on the weather. There are five major types of air masses that affect the weather in North America:

- Continental Arctic- originate in the Arctic and bring extremely cold temperatures
- Continental Polar- form just south of the Arctic Circle and create cold, dry conditions
- Maritime Polar- form over the northern parts of the Atlantic and Pacific Oceans and bring cool, moist weather
- Maritime Tropical- form over the southern part of the Atlantic and the Gulf of Mexico and bring warm temperatures and moisture
- Continental Tropical- forms over the desert in the southwestern United States and creates warm, dry weather

The weather in a particular area is greatly influenced by the season. Seasons are the four phases of the year caused by the Earth's revolution around the sun, marked by differences in weather patterns. Depending on their location on Earth, some areas experience the four seasons very distinctly, while in other areas, the weather remains more consistent.

The Universe and its Origins

The Earth is just one among many bodies in the universe. The universe is thought to be approximately 20 billion years old. The Big Bang Theory states that the universe was created when a large collection of matter exploded, sending pieces of it that would become the planets, stars and other bodies expanding outward.

Galaxies

Galaxies are systems of stars. The Earth belongs to the Milky Way Galaxy.

Astronomers (scientists who study celestial bodies) keep track of stars by organizing them into constellations.

Solar Systems

Within galaxies are solar systems, which consist of planets and other bodies orbiting a star. Our solar system consists of eight planets that orbit around the sun in elliptical patterns—Mercury, Venus, Earth, Mars, Jupiter, Saturn, Uranus, and Neptune—as well as their moons, asteroids, and other celestial objects.

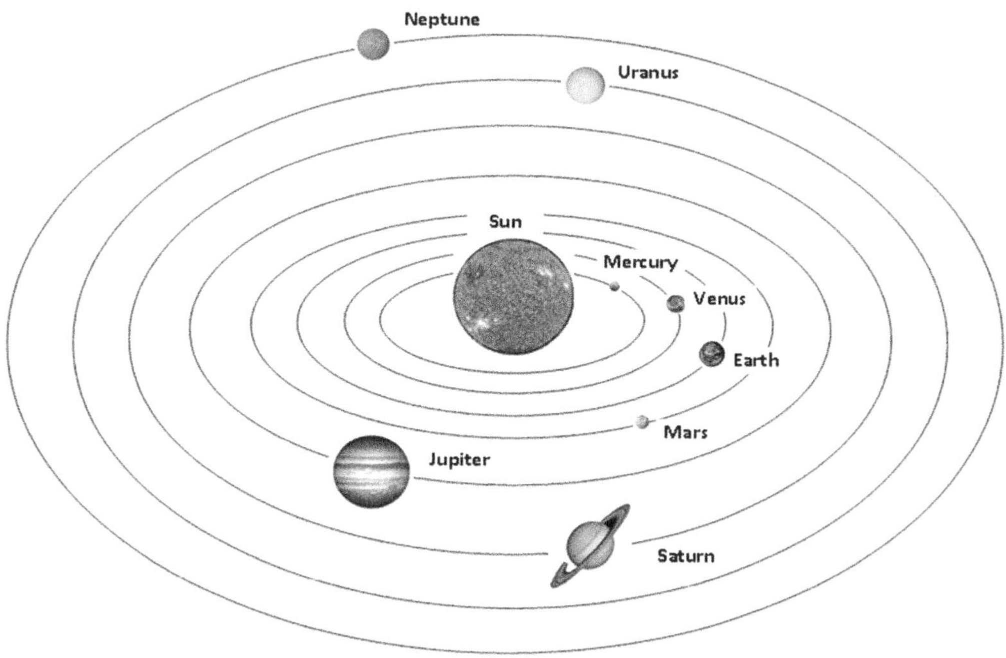

Moons

Moons revolve around planets, held in orbit by gravity. Some planets have more than one moon, but the Earth only has one, known as the Moon.

It takes the Moon 28 days to revolve around the Earth. The Moon does not give off any light of its own, but reflects light from the sun. Depending on the position of the Moon and the Earth in relationship to the sun, the Moon looks different from Earth at different times of the month. These are called the phases of the Moon.

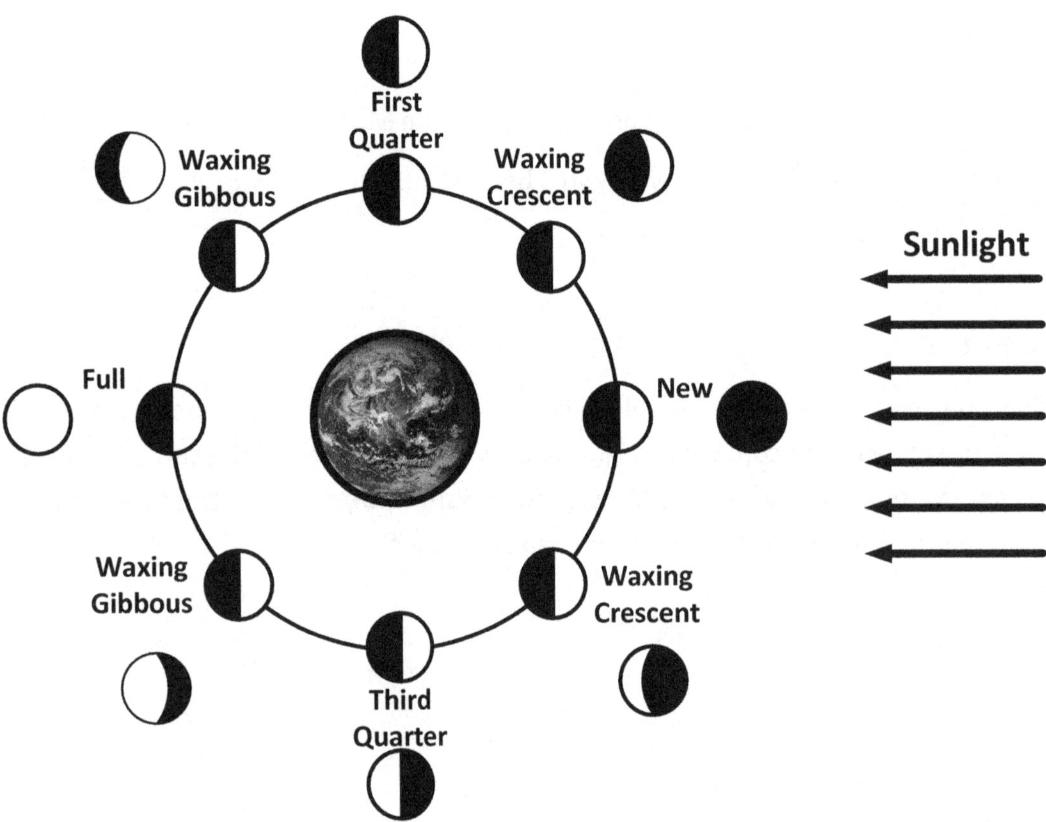

Eclipses are special events in which the sun, Moon, and Earth all line up in a direct path.

In a **solar eclipse**, the Moon is directly between the sun and the Earth and casts a shadow on the Earth's surface.

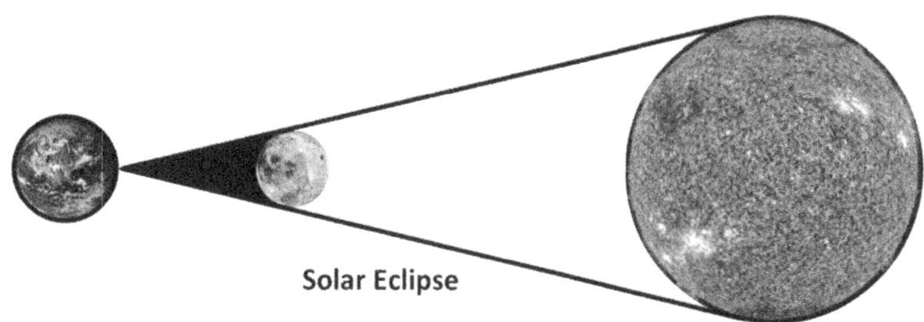

In a **lunar eclipse**, the Earth is directly between the sun and the Moon, blocking light from hitting the Moon.

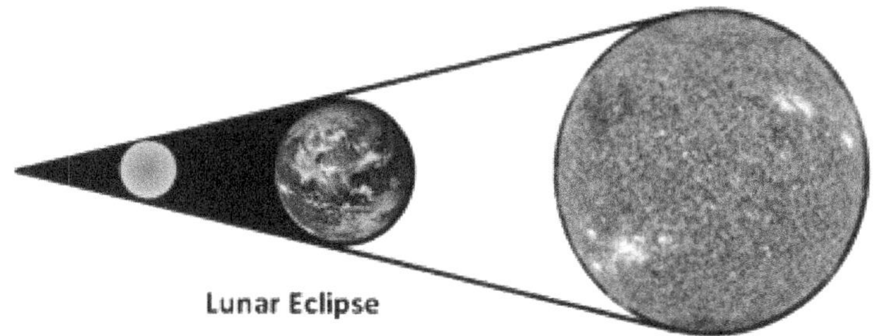

Other Celestial Objects

There are other objects in space besides stars, planets, and moons. Some of these include:

- **Asteroids**- large rocky objects in space; there is a large asteroid belt between Mars and Jupiter
- **Meteoroid**s- smaller rocky or metallic objects travelling through space
- **Meteorites**- meteoroids that enter Earth's atmosphere
- **Meteors**- streaks of light that trail behind meteorites as they burn in Earth's atmosphere
- **Comets**- icy bodies that form tails as they near the sun

The Foundations of Scientific Thought

This section covers the nature and history of scientific inquiry, as well as the ways in which the cultural and political climate can affect scientific progress in positive and negative ways.

Topics Addressed:

1. The Development of Scientific Thinking
2. Factors that Affect Scientific Progress

The Nature and Goals of Science

Science is the study of the natural world through observation and experimentation. There are many reasons that people undertake scientific inquiry. Two of the major motivations for scientific exploration are:

- Desire to satisfy curiosity about the world
- Seeking practical applications of science that will benefit humanity

There are certain traits that scientists in any field tend to have in common that relate to the way they think about the world and about their work. Scientific thinking tends to involve:

- A natural curiosity about how things work
- Openness to new ideas
- An appropriate amount of skepticism and the refusal to take things at face value without investigation
- Willingness to work in cooperation with others

The Dynamic Nature of Science

Science is a field that is constantly changing as humans learn more and more about the world. Things that were considered the "truth" 1,000 or even 10 years ago may no longer hold true as new information comes to light. Scientific knowledge is constantly being revised as new theories are tested, as scientists build upon the work of their predecessors, and as technology allows for experimentation methods that were previously unavailable.

Some components of the dynamic nature of science include:

- **Durability**- the ability of something to stand the test of time
- **Tentativeness**- the idea that something has been made or done on a trial basis or as an experiment, or is not final or conclusive

- **Reliance on evidence**- Scientists must rely on evidence to back up their claims. They must also be willing to adjust previously held notions when new evidence comes to light.
- **Replication**- the idea that a valid experiment must have reproducibility and that when attempted again, the experiment would yield the same conclusions; replication is important for new scientific findings to be accepted

Major Historical Developments in Science

Science is constantly evolving, but some of the major scientists in history and their contributions are listed in the table below.

Scientist	Major Areas of Contribution
Nicolas Copernicus	Heliocentric model of the solar system
Galileo Galilei	Heliocentric model of the solar system; discovered moons of Jupiter; invented telescope
Johannes Kepler	Laws of Planetary Motion
Leonardo da Vinci	Human anatomy; theorized about flight
Isaac Newton	Gravity, Laws of Motion
Charles Darwin	Natural selection and evolutionary biology
Gregor Mendel	Genetics
Louis Pasteur	Microorganisms
Thomas Edison	Light bulb; DC electricity
Pierre and Marie Curie	Radioactivity
Nikola Tesla	Physics, engineering, AC electricity
James Watson and Francis Crick	DNA
Albert Einstein	Theoretical physics, including the theory of relativity

Factors that Affect Scientific Progress

Scientific progress can either be helped or hindered by society. Throughout history, there have been periods and cultures that have encouraged scientific inquiry and those that have impeded its progress.

Scientific progress is aided by factors such as:

- Political support
- Popular support
- Funding
- Availability of talent
- Educational opportunity
- Entrepreneurship

Scientific progress can experience resistance due to:

- Political opposition or a slow bureaucratic system
- Lack of funding
- Religious or ethical opposition
- Lack of educational opportunity

Scientific Inquiry and Experimentation

This section covers the methods and processes of scientific experimentation, as well the applications of science in the areas of engineering and technology.

Topics Addressed:

1. Concepts and Processes of Scientific Experimentation
2. Health and Safety Measures
3. The Relationships Among Science, Technology, and Engineering
4. Processes of Engineering Design

Science is the process by which we gain new knowledge of how the world works. The process is one of inquiry, wherein people ask questions about the world and make observations and perform experiments in order to find the answers to those questions.

Scientific Investigations

Scientific investigations can come in many forms, but the three major types are experiments, observations, and surveys.

- An **experiment** is a test performed under controlled conditions. Experiments can be conducted to test a hypothesis, to demonstrate something already known, or to try something new.
- **Observation** is watching an event very meticulously and keeping an account of what you see.
- A **survey** is used to gather information from a sampling of people by asking them all the same set of questions.

The Scientific Method

The main process used in scientific inquiry is known as the Scientific Method. This lays out the proper steps for scientific investigations.

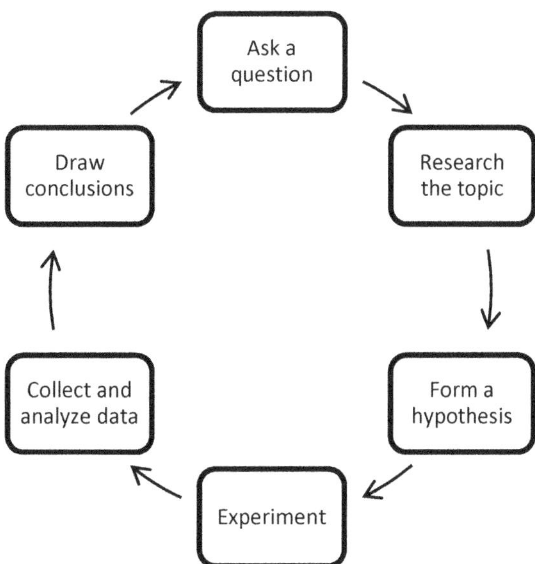

Collecting and Measuring Data

The methods used to collect data are very important in science. For scientific research to be considered reputable, the methods used to obtain the results must be reported along with the result and must be found to be honest and thorough.

Some important components of data collection include:

- Identifying and controlling variables
- Careful observation
- The accurate recording of measurement data using appropriate tools

Analyzing and Representing Data

Once data has been collected from an experiment, a scientist needs a way to show that data and then analyze it and allow it to be analyzed by others. Data representation can take many forms depending on the experiment, but may include graphs, tables, charts, and/or narration.

Analysis of the data involves looking for patterns, checking the data against the hypothesis behind the experiment, and drawing logical conclusions. In some cases, the original hypothesis may be revised and become the subject of further experimentation.

Health and Safety Measures

An important consideration in the science classroom is safety. Scientific experiments and demonstrations can involve potentially dangerous equipment and substances. Equipment and materials must be properly stored and handled and students must be taught safe and appropriate behavior in laboratory settings. Some safety considerations for the classroom include:

- Students should be supervised at all times.
- Students should be taught to handle materials and equipment with caution.
- Instruct students on emergency procedures.
- Students should have appropriate safety gear, including goggles, gloves, and aprons where appropriate. Clothing (such as loose long sleeves), jewelry, and hair should be secured.
- Chemicals should be labeled.
- Hazardous chemicals should be kept in locked cabinets low to the ground.
- Keep bottles of liquid closed when not in use.
- A sink or eye-washing station should be readily available.
- A first aid kit should be ready and accessible.
- Know the location of and how to use a fire extinguisher.
- Dispose of materials in the appropriate receptacles.
- Students should be taught the appropriate way to handle live animals.
- Hands should be washed after handling substances or animals.

The Relationships Among Science, Technology, and Engineering

Science, technology, and engineering go hand in hand. Scientific research and the design work of engineers are responsible for the vast array of technology we now enjoy. That advanced technology, in turn, allows science to continue and advance itself as it allows observation of phenomena and methods of experimentation never before possible.

Science has far-reaching implications for society as it shapes how we understand the world and creates the technology we use on a daily basis. It has implications for the shaping of cultural, economic, and political life throughout the world.

Careers in science are plentiful and include a wide variety of areas, including medicine, engineering, environmental science, astronomy, geology, computer science, science education, meteorology, biochemistry, and so many more. Students should be introduced to practical applications and careers in science in order to maintain a real world connection with the content they are learning.

Processes of Engineering Design

When engineers design, their work goes through several stages of development. The major stages in the engineering design process are:

1. Research- The engineer conducts background research about the subject at hand, often looking at previous work in the field and the designs of others working on similar projects.
2. Design and Development- This is the stage during which the engineer actually creates and executes a plan for the material, structure, or system being designed.
3. Testing- During the testing phase, the design is put into use under controlled circumstances and monitored.
4. Evaluation and Redesign- The results of the testing process are analyzed and necessary revisions to the design are made based on the findings of the evaluation.

Mathematics

Knowledge of mathematics is foundational for student success. Students develop skills in mathematical problem-solving that transfer to many real world applications and career fields.

Test Structure

The Mathematics subtest consists of 45 multiple choice questions and 1 open response question. Within Mathematics, there are five major subcategories with which you must be familiar:

A. Numbers and Operations (41% of Mathematics subtest)

B. Functions and Algebra (22% of Mathematics subtest)

C. Geometry and Measurement (18% of Mathematics subtest)

D. Statistics and Probability (16% of Mathematics subtest)

E. Integration of Knowledge and Understanding (open response question worth 12% of Mathematics subtest)

Each subcategory is divided into topics, which include the skills you must be able to demonstrate on the exam.

Numbers and Operations

This section covers number theory, the four major operations, and basic mathematical concepts and strategies which will lay the foundation for students' future mathematical learning. It accounts for 41% of the Mathematics subtest.

Topics Addressed:

1. Number Systems and Place Value
2. Types of Numbers
3. Number Theory
4. Numerical Operations

Number Systems and Place Value

Basic Number Systems

There are several basic categories of numbers.

- **Natural numbers** are those numbers we typically use to count (1, 2, 3...)
- **Whole numbers** are the natural numbers and zero (0, 1, 2, 3...)
- **Integers** are whole numbers and their corresponding negatives (.. -3, -2, -1, 0, 1, 2, 3...)
- **Fractions** are portions of integers, expressed with a numerator and a denominator

  (¼, ½, etc.)
- **Decimals** are portions of integers, expressed as numbers following a decimal point

  (0.5, 0.67, etc.)
- **Even numbers** are integers divisible by two (...-6, -4, -2, 2, 4, 6...)
- **Odd numbers** are integers not divisible by two(... -7, -5, -3, 3, 5, 7...)
- **Rational numbers** are all integers and fractions
- **Irrational numbers** are any numbers that cannot be expressed as fractions, such as an infinite, non-repeating decimal
- **Exponents** are numbers that raise another number to a power, making it multiply by itself a certain number of times ($3^2 = 3 \times 3 = 9$, etc.)
- **Roots-** the root of a number *x* is another number such that when the number is multiplied by itself a given number of times, it equals *x* ($\sqrt{4} = 2$, etc.)

Place Value

Place value is a way of organizing numbers based on groupings of ten. The place value in which a digit lays conveys how many groups of ten (or one hundred, or one thousand, etc.) it represents. Place value is also used in decimals.

Whole Numbers						
Millions	Hundred Thousands	Ten Thousands	Thousands	Hundreds	Tens	Units
1,000,000	100,000	10,000	1,000	100	10	1
2,478,390	2,**4**78,390	2,4**7**8,390	2,47**8**,390	2,478,**3**90	2,478,3**9**0	2,478,39**0**

Decimals					
Tenths	Hundredths	Thousandths	Ten Thousandths	Hundred Thousandths	Millionths
.1	.01	.001	.0001	.00001	.000001
.**2**37894	.2**3**7894	.23**7**894	.237**8**94	.2378**9**4	.23789**4**

Scientific Notation and Expanded Form

There are also different ways to write out the same number so that it looks different and is in a standardized form. Scientific notation and expanded form are two different ways of writing numbers that are both based on place value in a base-ten system

Scientific notation puts all numbers in a standard form by changing them so that there is only one place value before a decimal point and then the number is written in terms of multiplication by 10 to a power.

Examples: 321 becomes 3.21×10^2

2,250.75 becomes 2.25075×10^3

0.62 becomes 6.2×10^{-1}

Expanded form breaks a number up into an addition expression based on the place value of each digit.

Examples: 748 becomes 700 + 40 + 8

2,389 becomes 2,000 + 300 + 80 + 9

Precision and Accuracy

Precision and accuracy are ways of describing measurement data.

Precision is how close measured values are to each other.

Accuracy is how close a measured value is to an actual (true) value.

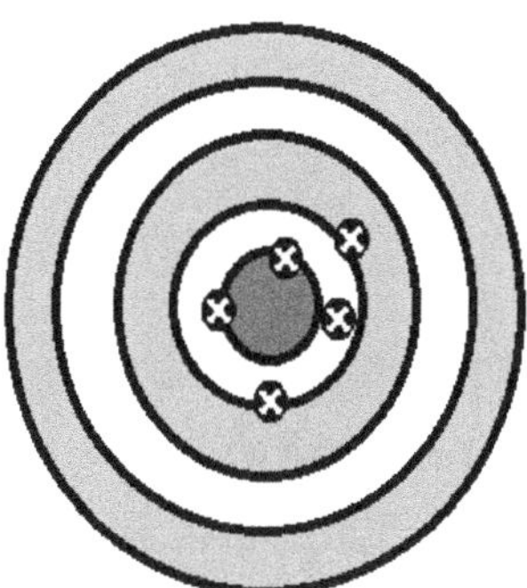

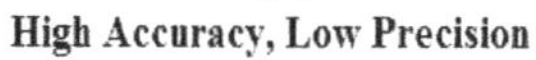

High Accuracy, Low Precision

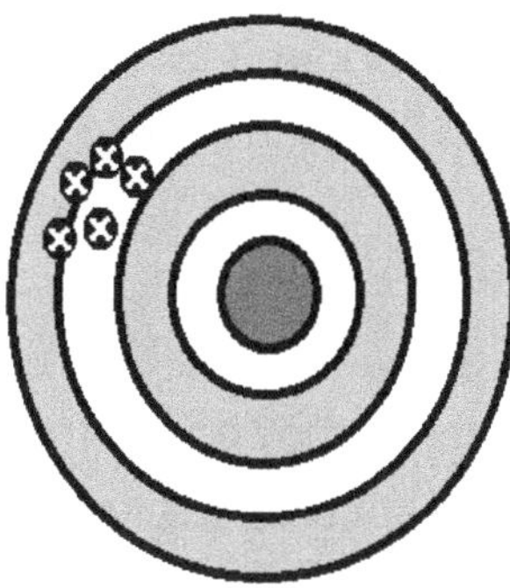

High Precision, Low Accuracy

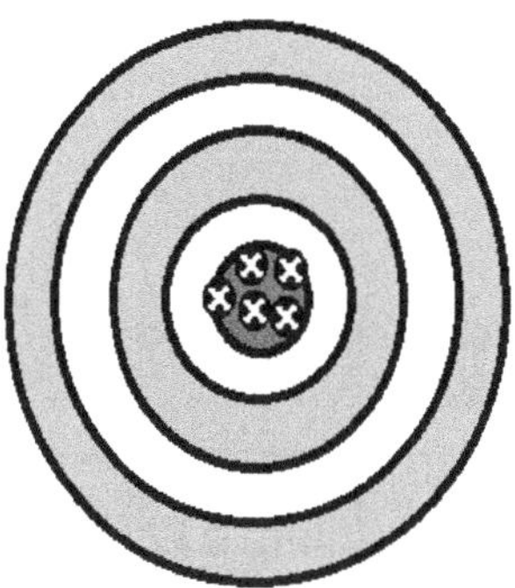

High Precision, High Accuracy

Estimation

Estimation provides a close guess as to a value. An exact number is not always necessary and estimation can be a time-saving skill for everyday calculations such as product costs, how much should be left for a tip, and quantity estimations.

One type of estimation is **rounding**, which is arriving at a close value to a given number based on place value. You can round to any place value.

The rule for rounding is to look one place to the right of the place value you want to round to. If that digit is five or higher, round up. If it is less than five, round down.

Example:

Number	Roundest to the Nearest Ten	Rounded to the Nearest Hundred	Rounded to the Nearest Thousand
3,583	3,580	3,600	4,000
6,149	6,150	6,100	6,000

Integers and Fractions

Fractions are used to represent a part of a whole. **Integers** are numbers that do not contain fractional parts (whole numbers and their negatives).

Students should have an understanding of the meaning of fractions and be able to solve problems with the four basic operations involving fractions.

Representing Fractions

Visuals are often used to help students understand fractions. Creating a visual representation of a fraction involves splitting a whole into equivalent parts and indicating (usually through shading) some of those parts as the fractional pieces.

Example: $\frac{1}{4}$ can be represented as the shape below, which is split into four equal parts with one of them shaded.

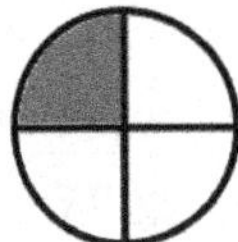

Students can be taught that the selected area represents the numerator of the fraction, and the total number of pieces represents the denominator of the fraction.

Improper Fractions and Mixed Numbers

When a fraction has a value that is greater than 1, it can either be expressed as an improper fraction or a mixed number.

An improper fraction has a numerator greater than the denominator (e.g., $\frac{22}{7}$).

A mixed number contains both a whole number and a fraction (e.g., $1\frac{1}{3}$).

To convert an improper fraction to a mixed number, divide the numerator by the denominator. The whole number portion of the quotient becomes the whole number of the mixed number, the remainder becomes the numerator of the new fraction, and the denominator remains the same.

Example: $\frac{22}{7} = 3\frac{1}{7}$

To convert a mixed number to an improper fraction, multiply the denominator by the whole number and add the numerator. This total becomes the new numerator and the denominator remains the same.

Example: $1\frac{1}{3} = \frac{4}{3}$

Numerical Representations

Translating Mathematical Language

Mathematical problem-solving requires knowledge of such concepts as representation, variables, and arithmetic operations. In order to solve problems, students will need to be comfortable with the vocabulary associated with the arithmetic operations. This is especially important in word problems where students will need to deduce the operation necessary to solve without being able to see the symbol for the operation.

Addition	Subtraction	Multiplication	Division
Add	*Subtract*	*Multiply*	*Divide*
Sum	*Difference*	*Product*	*Quotient*
More than	*Less than*	*Total*	*Distribute*
Plus	*Minus*	*Times*	*Per*
In addition	*Diminished*		
Increased	*Decreased*		
All together	*Remove*		
Total	*Take away*		
And	*Deduct*		

Equivalence

Equivalence is being equal in value. The same value can take on many different forms. For example. a fraction can also be expressed as a decimal that is equal in value.

Many mathematical situations will require students to work with the concept of equivalence and to translate from one equivalent form of a number to another. This can include generating equivalent fractions; simplifying expressions; and converting between fractions, decimals, and percents.

Example:

Fraction(s)	Decimal	Percent
$\frac{1}{4}, \frac{2}{8},$ etc.	0.25	25%
$\frac{1}{2}, \frac{2}{4},$ etc.	0.5	50%

Graphic Representations

Quantitative information can be displayed visually with the use of charts and graphs. There are several common types of charts and graphs with which elementary students should be familiar.

Pictographs

Pictographs use pictures or symbols to represent pieces of data. A symbol may represent one item or a key may indicate that each symbol represents more than one item. Quantities of each item are obtained by counting the symbols.

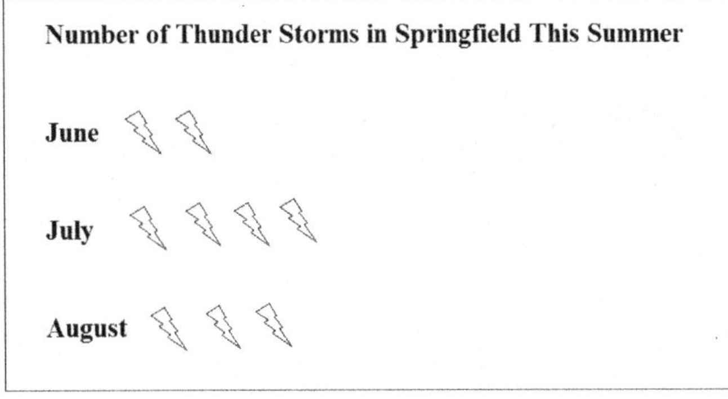

Bar Graphs

Bar graphs use bars to represent quantities. The quantity represented by each bar is obtained by reading the height of the bar.

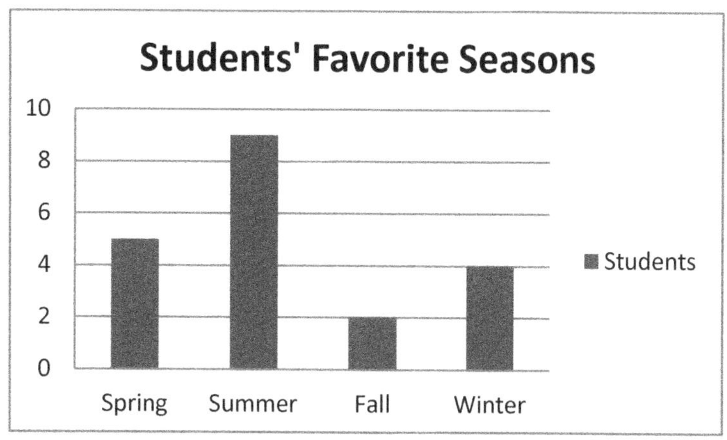

Pie Graphs

Pie graphs are used to show information in relation to a whole. The circle represents a whole and is divided into segments to represent the portions. The portions are usually shown in percentages.

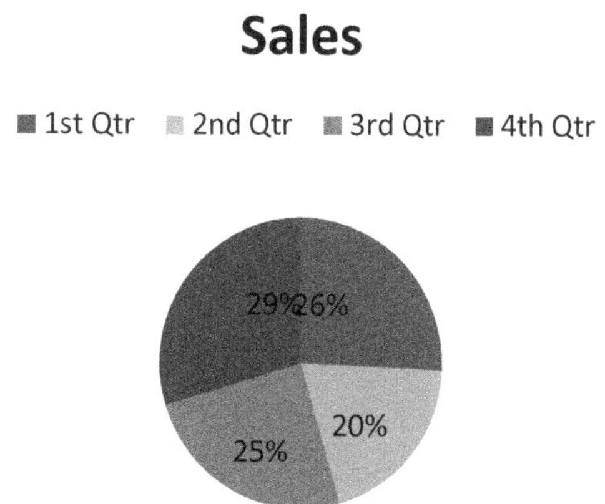

Line Graphs

Line graphs use lines to connect data points and are used to show change over time.

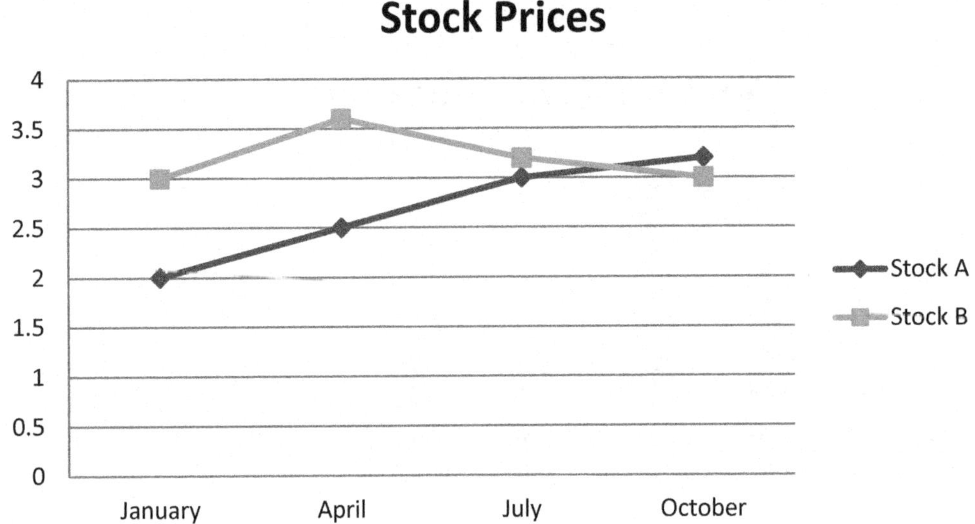

Factors

Factors are whole numbers that are multiplied together to get a product.

Example: The factors of 16 are 1, 2, 4, 8, and 16.

The processing of breaking a number down into its factors is called **factoring**.

Prime and Composite Numbers

Whole numbers can be classified by how many factors they have as either being prime or composite numbers.

- **Prime numbers** are those numbers (other than zero and one) that have only two factors—themselves and 1

  2, 3, 5, 7, 11...

- **Composite numbers** are any positive integers that are not prime, meaning they have more than two factors

  4, 6, 8, 9, 10...

Prime factorization involves factoring a number and then factoring the factors, if necessary, until all factors are prime and multiply together to equal the original number. One way of performing prime factorization is by using a **factor tree**.

Example: The prime factorization of 24 is 3 x 2 x 2 x 2.

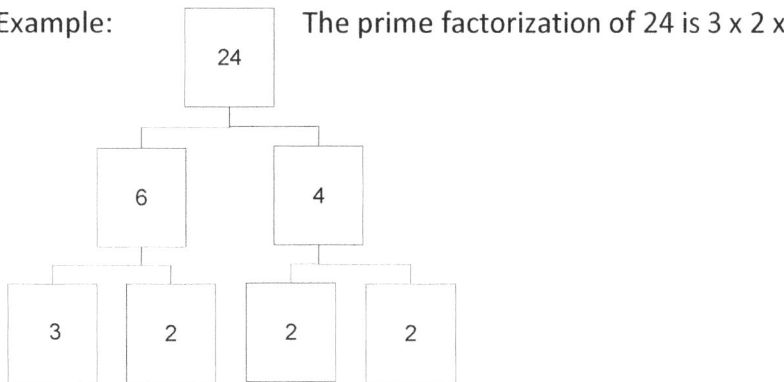

Greatest Common Factor

When comparing the factors of two numbers, the largest factor that they have in common in called the **Greatest Common Factor (GCF)**.

Example:

- Factors of 20: 1, 2, **4**, 5, 10, 20
- Factors of 24: 1, 2, 3, **4**, 6, 8, 12, 24

GCF: 4

Multiples

Multiples are the result of multiplying a number by whole numbers.

Example:

- The multiples of 4 are 4, 8, 12, 16, 20, 24...

Least Common Multiple

When comparing the multiples of two numbers, the smallest multiple that they have in common is called the **Least Common Multiple (LCM)**.

Example:

- Multiples of 3: 3, 6, 9, 12, **15**, 18, 21...
- Multiples of 5: 5, 10, **15**, 20, 25, 30...

LCM: 15

The four basic operations—addition, subtraction, multiplication, and division—serve as the basis for all mathematical processes.

Addition

Addition is bringing two or more numbers (or objects) together to make a new total called a **sum**. A common method used in addition is regrouping by carrying. When adding vertically, add each place value individually, starting on the right and moving left. If any single place value sums to a number greater than 10, keep the value over 10 in that place value and carry the tens place to the next column to be added into that place value.

Example

$$\begin{array}{r} 25 \\ 18 \\ \underline{+\ 11} \end{array}$$

$$\begin{array}{r} 2\mathbf{5} \\ 1\mathbf{8} \\ \underline{+\ 1\mathbf{1}} \end{array}$$

First, add the ones place column.

$$\begin{array}{r} 1 \\ 25 \\ 18 \\ \underline{+\ 11} \\ 54 \end{array}$$

The sum of those numbers is 14, which is larger than 10. To regroup, write the 4 in the ones column of the answer space, and move the 1 to the tens place. It will be added in there for a total of 54.

Subtraction

Subtraction is taking numbers (or objects) away from a group to create a new total, called a **difference**. A common method used in subtraction is regrouping by borrowing. When subtracting vertically, subtract each place value individually, moving from right to left. If ever the top number (the one you are subtracting *from*) is smaller than the bottom number (the one being subtracted), you will need to borrow. To borrow, add 10 to the digit you were trying to subtract from, then subtract 1 from the next place to the left to compensate.

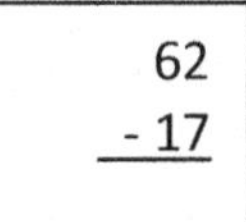

Example

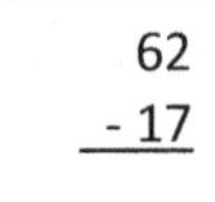

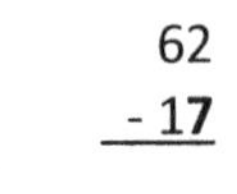

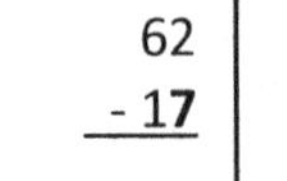

Start with the ones column.

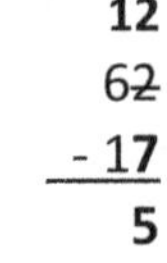

Notice that the 2 is not large enough to subtract the 7 from it. This means we will need to borrow.

Borrow making the

5 12
~~62~~
- 17
45

from the tens column by subtracting 1 from the top number, 6 into a 5. Then subtract the tens column. The answer is 45.

Multiplication

Multiplication is adding a number to itself a certain number of times. It is ultimately a shortcut to repeated addition. Multiplication quantifies equal groups of things.

The two numbers in a multiplication problem are called the multiplicand and the multiplier. The answer is called the **product**. The typical process for multiplication involves multiplying the multiplicand by each digit of the multiplier, then adding the results to get the product.

Example

```
  42
x 13
```

```
  42
x 13
 126
```

Start by multiplying the multiplicand (42) by the ones place of the multiplier. 4 x 3 = 12 and 2 x 3 =6

```
  42
x 13
 126
 420
```

Then, multiply 42 by the tens place of the multiplier, using a 0 to hold the place value in the ones.

2 x 1 = 2 and 4 x 1 = 4

```
  42
x 13
 126
+420
 546
```

Finally, add these results to get the final product of 546.

Division

Division is splitting a number into equal groups. The number being divided is the **dividend**, the number it is divided by is the **divisor**, and the answer is the **quotient**.

In division, dividing moves in place values from left to right. Any leftovers that do not divide evenly into the dividend become either a remainder, fraction, or decimal.

Example

```
5|257
```

```
  5
5|257
```

In this example, 257 is the dividend and 5 is the divisor. Move from left to right in the place values of the dividend. 5 cannot divide into 2.

```
  5
5|257
```

Expand to the right and look at the first two digits, 25.

5 *does* divide evenly into 25 (5 times).

```
  51 R2
5|257
 -5
  2
```

Now, move to the right again. 5 goes into 7 with a remainder of 2. To divide without remainders, you would add on decimal places until the division comes out evenly. In this case, the result would be 51.4

Note: There are many methods for division other than the long division shown, but the basic elements are still the same.

Modeling the Four Operations

Addition and Subtraction Models

Addition can be modeled as a "**put-together**" problem, with either an unknown addend or an unknown sum. Visual models can be used to show the parts being put together to form a total.

Example: *There are 2 oranges and 3 bananas in a fruit bowl. How many pieces of fruit are there all together?*

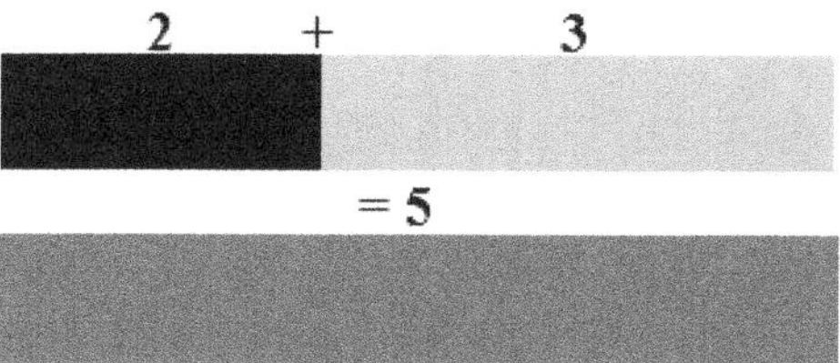

There are 5 pieces of fruit all together.

Subtraction can be modeled as a "**take-apart**" problem, with either an unknown minuend, an unknown subtrahend, or an unknown difference. Visual models can be used to show that subtraction means splitting a whole into component parts.

Example: *8 students were asked whether they like dogs or cats better. 5 students picked dogs. How many students picked cats?*

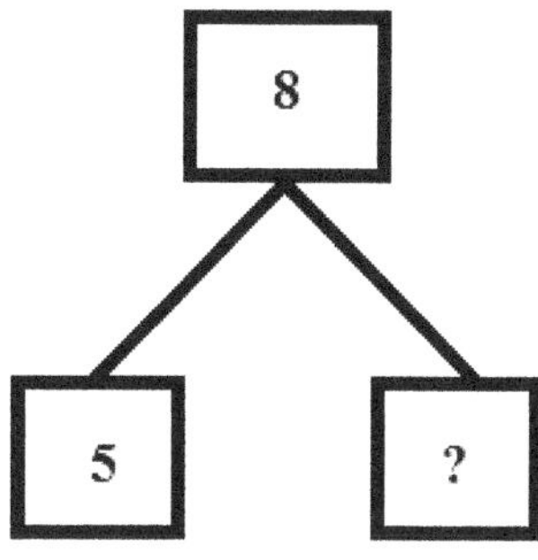

3 students picked cats.

Multiplication and Area Models

An **array** is one way to model a multiplication problem visually. One factor is shown vertically and the other horizontally.

Example: 4 x 3 = 12 can be modeled as an array like this:

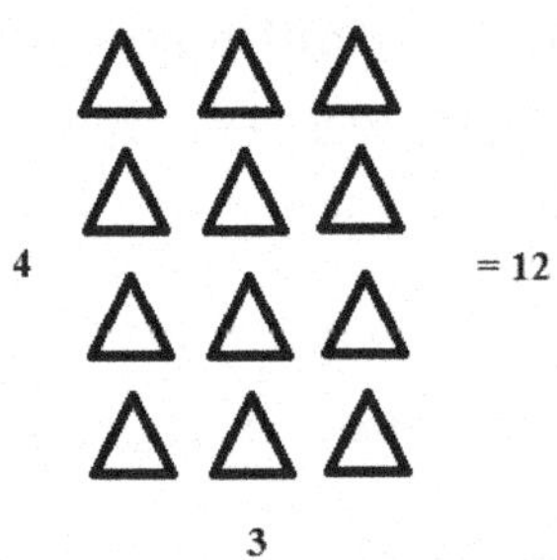

This can also be used to relate to calculating the area of rectangles as it is similar to **tiling**, wherein a rectangle is divided into unit squares which can be counted to find the area.

Example: To find the area of a rectangle that measures 8 units by 4 units using tiling, divide the rectangle into unit squares and count them to find the area.

8

4

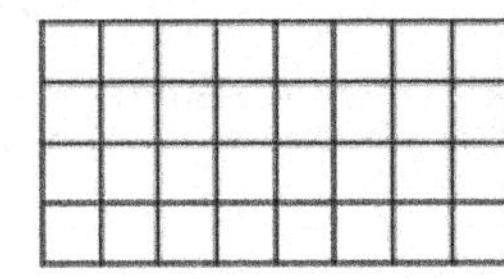

8 x 4 = 32 units^2

Division Models

There are two main types of division problems:

- **Measurement division** is needed when students know how many objects are in each group but do not know how many groups there are
- **Partitive division** is needed when students know how many groups there need to be but not how many objects will be in each group

Visual models can be used to understand either type of division problem as splitting objects into equal groupings.

Example: *Jason is placing 6 cookies into bags to keep them fresh. If he puts 3 cookies in each bag, how many bags will he fill?*

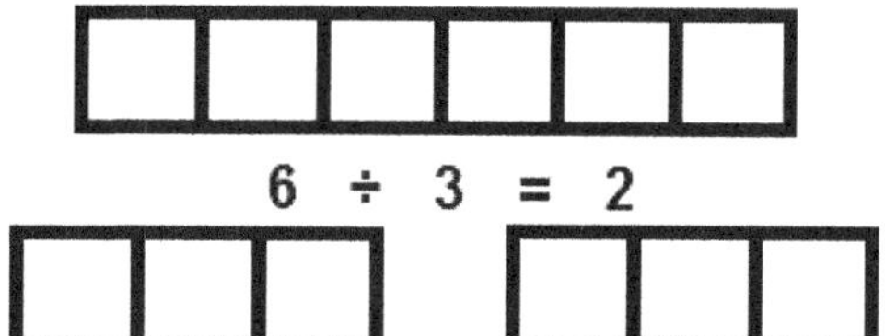

He will fill 2 bags.

Properties of Numbers and Operations

The Commutative, Distributive, and Associative Properties

Basic operations have special properties that govern how they work and can make them easier to solve.

Property	Applies To	Description	Example
Commutative Property	Addition and Multiplication	The order of the numbers being added or multiplied does not affect final result	1 + 3 = 3 + 1 2 x 5 = 5 x 2
Distributive Property	Multiplication	*a(b + c) = ab + ac* Multiplication in front of parenthesis can be distributed to each term within the parentheses.	2(3+1) = 2 x 3 + 2 x 1 = 6 + 2 = 8 This yields the same result as 2(3+1) = 2(4) = 8

Associative Property	Addition and Multiplication	If the operations are all the same (all addition or all multiplication) the terms can be regrouped by moving the parentheses. $(a + b) + c = a + (b + c)$ $a(bc) = (ab)c$	Addition: (1 + 2) + 3 = 3 + 3 = 6 1 + (2 + 3) = 1 + 5 = 6 Multiplication: $3(4y) = 12y$ $(3 \times 4)y = 12y$

Order of Operations

When an equation has more than one of these operations in it, the operations must be performed in a certain order. The order can be remembered with the acronym PEMDAS, which stands for:

- **Parentheses**- Complete any operations enclosed within parentheses first. If more than one operation is inside the parentheses, perform the operations within the parentheses in PEMDAS order, then proceed with the operations outside the parentheses.
- **Exponents**- Deal with any exponents next.
- **Multiplication/Division**- Multiplication and division can be done in the same step as one another.
- **Addition/Subtraction**- Addition and subtraction can be done in the same step as one another.

Special Properties of Zero and One

Zero and one have their own special properties that no other numbers possess.

Properties of Zero

- *Addition property of zero*- Adding 0 to a number does not change the number's value.

  $x + 0 = x$

- *Multiplication property of zero*- Any number multiplied by 0 equals 0

  $0x = 0$

- *Additive inverse*- The sum of any number and its additive inverse is 0

$x + -x = 0$

- *Powers of zero-* 0 raised to any power equals 0

  $0^x = 0$

- *Zero as a dividend-* Dividing 0 by any number results in a quotient of 0

  $0 \div x = 0$

- *Division by zero-* Dividing any number by 0 results in a quotient that is undefined

  $x \div 0 =$ undefined

Properties of One

- *Multiplication property of one-* Multiplying a number by 1 does not change the number's value.

  $1x = x$

- *Multiplicative inverse-* The product of any number and its multiplicative inverse is 1

  $x(\frac{1}{x}) = 1$

- *Powers of one-* 1 raised to any power equals 1

  $1^x = 1$

- *Quotient of one-* Any number (other than 0) divided by itself equals 1

  $x \div x = 1$

Additive and Multiplicative Inverses

An **additive inverse** of a number is its equal opposite such that when the two are added together, they will equal 0. For example:

Number	Additive Inverse
1	-1
-25	25
x	$-x$

The **multiplicative inverse** of a number is the reciprocal of the number such that when the two are multiplied, they equal 1. For example:

Number	Multiplicative Inverse
5	1/5
1/2	2
x	$1/x$

Absolute Value

A related concept is that of **absolute value**, a number's distance from 0. Absolute value is always positive. If the number is greater than 0, it is its own absolute value. If negative, its additive inverse (the positive equivalent of itself) is its absolute value. For example:

Number	Absolute Value
5	5
-10	10
x	x
$-x$	x

Laws of Exponents

The following chart lays out the basic rules governing the use of exponents.

Types of Laws	Law	Example
Product Rules	$a^n \cdot a^m = a^{n+m}$	$2^2 \cdot 2^3 = 2^{2+3} = 32$
	$a^n \cdot b^n = (a \cdot b)^n$	$2^2 \cdot 3^2 = (2 \cdot 3)^2 = 36$
Quotient Rules	$a^n / a^m = a^{n-m}$	$2^5 / 2^3 = 2^{5-3} = 4$
	$a^n / b^n = (a / b)^n$	$4^3 / 2^3 = (4/2)^3 = 8$
Power Rules	$(b^n)^m = b^{n \cdot m}$	$(2^3)^4 = 2^{3 \cdot 4} = 4096$
	${}^m\sqrt{}(b^n) = b^{n/m}$	${}^2\sqrt{}(2^4) = 2^{4/2} = 4$

Negative Exponents	$b^{-n} = 1 / b^n$	$2^{-3} = 1/2^3 = 0.125$
Zero Rules	$b^0 = 1$	$9^0 = 1$
	$0^n = 0$, for $n>0$	$0^3 = 0$
One Rules	$b^1 = b$	$7^1 = 7$
	$1^n = 1$	$1^4 = 1$

Performing Operations on Fractions

Adding and Subtracting Fractions

To add and subtract fractions with like denominators, leave the denominator alone and add or subtract the numerators.

Example: $\frac{1}{5} + \frac{3}{5} = \frac{4}{5}$

To add or subtract fractions with unlike denominators, change the fractions to equivalent ones with a common denominator, then add or subtract the numerators.

Example: $\frac{1}{5} + \frac{2}{3} =$

$\frac{3}{15} + \frac{10}{15} = \frac{13}{15}$

Multiplying and Dividing Fractions

To multiply fractions, multiply across, combining the numerators to form a new numerator and the denominators to form a new denominator.

Example: $\frac{1}{4} \text{ x } \frac{3}{5} = \frac{3}{20}$

To divide fractions, change the second fraction to its reciprocal (switch the numerator and denominator) and multiply.

Example: $\frac{2}{3} \div \frac{3}{5} =$

$\frac{2}{3} \text{ x } \frac{5}{3} = \frac{10}{9} \text{ (or } 1\frac{1}{9}\text{)}$

Comparing Fractions

When comparing fractions with like denominators, the fraction with the larger numerator has the greater value.

Example: $\frac{2}{3} > \frac{1}{3}$

When comparing fractions with the same numerator but different denominators, the fraction with the smaller denominator has the greater value.

Example: $\frac{2}{3} > \frac{2}{5}$

When comparing fractions that have neither the same numerators nor denominators, convert the fractions so that they have a common denominator and then compare the numerators as before.

Example: To compare $\frac{3}{4}$ and $\frac{2}{3}$, first change the fractions so that they have a common denominator, then compare the numerators.

$\frac{9}{12} > \frac{8}{12}$ therefore $\frac{3}{4} > \frac{2}{3}$.

Problem-Solving Strategies

There are many different methods for solving mathematical problems. No single method will be the most effective for every student on every problem. Some of the strategies students will employ include:

- Modeling
- Estimation
- Using algorithms
- Mental math

- Looking for patterns
- Calculator use

When problem-solving, it is important for students to be able to recognize the reasonableness of results. When they find a solution, they should check to see if their answer makes sense—if the number they have arrived at seems reasonable based on the parameters of the problem. This is a means of self-check.

Mathematical investigations are problems which ask students to formulate their own conjectures, test those conjectures, modify them if need be, and draw conclusions. Engaging in mathematical investigations requires students to employ critical thinking skills, to hypothesize, to collect data, to synthesize information, and to analyze and evaluate.

Functions and Algebra

This section covers the fundamental concepts and processes of algebra, including equations, inequalities, and functions. This content accounts for 22% of the overall Mathematics subtest.

Topics Addressed:

1. Algebraic Concepts
2. Functions and Patterns
3. Linear Functions and Equations

Algebraic Language

Variables

A variable is a letter used to refer to an unknown quantity. Algebraic problem solving often requires solving to find the value of a variable.

Example: $2x = 12$

$x = 6$

Expressions

Expressions are mathematical phrases that can contain numbers, variables, and operations.

Equations

Equations are two mathematical expressions that are set equal to one another using an equals sign (=). An equation can also be called an **equality**.

When solving equations for a variable, operations performed to one side must be performed to the other.

There are several properties of equalities:

- Reflexive property- Every number is equal to itself.

  $x = x$

- Symmetric property- If a number is equal to another number, then the converse is also true.

  If $x = y$ then $y = x$.

- Transitive property- If number *a* is equal to number *b,* and number *b* is equal to number *c*, then number *a* is also equal to number *c*.

  If $x = y$ and $y = z$, then $x = z$.

- Substitution property- If two numbers are equal to one another, they are interchangeable.

  If $x = y$, then $x + z = y + z$

- Property of addition, subtraction, multiplication, and division- If two numbers are equal, they will remain equal if the same number is added to or subtracted from them, or if they are multiplied or divided by the same number.

  If $x = y$, then $x + z = y + z$ If $x = y$, then $xz = yz$

  If $x = y$, then $x - z = y - z$ If $x = y$, then $x/z = y/z$

Inequalities

An **inequality** is a comparison of two expressions. The two sides of the equation are separated by one of the following symbols:

- $<$ *less than*
- $>$ *greater than*
- $\leq$ *less than or equal to*
- $\geq$ *greater than or equal to*

When solving inequalities for a variable, operations performed to one side must be performed to the other. When adding or subtracting the same value from both sides, or when multiplying or dividing by a positive number on both sides, the inequality sign does not change. When multiplying or dividing by a negative number, the inequality sign is reversed.

Formulas

Formulas are standard equations with variables that follow specific rules and are used to solve specific types of problems. Below are several examples of fundamental algebraic formulas.

- Difference of two perfect squares

  $a^2 - b^2 = (a + b)(a - b)$

- Quadratic formula- a method of solving a quadratic equation ($ax^2 + bx + c = 0$)

  $x = \frac{-b \pm \sqrt{b^2 - 4ac}}{2a}$

- Pythagorean theorem- used to find a missing length of a right triangle

  $a^2 + b^2 = c^2$

- Distance formula- used to measure the distance between two points on a coordinate plane

  $d = \sqrt{(x_2 - x_1)^2 + (y_2 - y_1)^2}$

- Midpoint formula- used to find the midpoint between two points on a coordinate plane

  $\left(\frac{(x_2 + x_1)}{2}, \frac{(y_2 + y_1)}{2}\right)$

- Slope formula- used to find the slope of a line on a coordinate plane

  $m = \frac{y_2 - y_1}{x_2 - x_1}$

- Slope intercept formula- the equation of a straight line

  $y = mx + b$ where *m* is the slope and *b* is the y-intercept

Ratios, Proportions, and Percents

Ratios

A **ratio** is a way to compare two numbers.

> Example: If a parent has one son and three daughters, the ratio of sons to daughters would be one to three.

A ratio can be expressed in words, as a fraction, or as two numbers separated by a colon. The ratio "one to three" is the same as "$\frac{1}{3}$" is the same as "1:3."

Proportions

A **proportion** is two ratios set equal to each other. Proportions are often expressed as two fractions with an equals sign between them.

> Example: $\frac{1}{3} = \frac{2}{6}$

Proportions that include an unknown can be solved by cross-multiplying.

Example: The ratio of cats to dogs in a pet is 3 to 2. If there are 12 cats, how many dogs are there?

$$\frac{3}{2} = \frac{12}{x}$$

$3x = 12 \times 2$

$3x = 24$

$x = 8$

There are 8 dogs in the pet store.

Percents

Percents convey a ratio out of 100. Percents are represented with a percentage symbol (%). The percentage formula is:

$$\frac{\%}{100} = \frac{part}{whole}$$

It is solved by cross-multiplying.

Example: What is 20% of 50?

$$\frac{20}{100} = \frac{x}{50}$$

$100x = 1{,}000$

$x = 10$

Functions and Patterns

Functions

Functions are algebraic equations that have an input (*x*) and an output (*f(x)*). In a function, each input value corresponds with exactly one output value. At the elementary level, functions are often expressed using tables and are then sometimes graphed.

Example:

Input	Output
2	5
3	6
15	18
21	24

Rule: Add 3

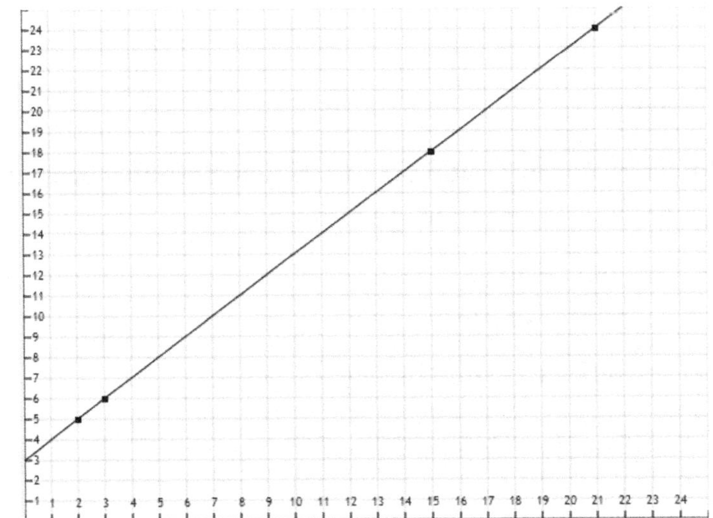

You can tell whether or not a graph shows a function by using the **vertical line test**. If a vertical line would only pass through the graph once, it is a function.

Functions whose data points form a straight-line graph are known as **linear functions**. Those that do not form a straight line are called **non-linear functions**.

Numerical Patterns

Numerical patterns are sets of numbers that follow a rule that governs the relationship between the numbers and dictates what number will come next in the set. Numerical patterns require students to analyze a set of numbers, discover the relationship between them, and articulate the pattern as a general rule that will work to the *n*th term in the series. Some examples of common number patterns are:

Pattern Name	Description	Example
Arithmetic Sequence	The same value is added each time	1, 5, 9, 13, 17, 21... (add 4 each time)
Geometric Sequence	The same value is multiplied each time	1, 3, 9, 27, 81... (multiply by 3 each time)
Squares	Square each number (n^2)	1, 4, 9, 16, 25...
Cubes	Cube each number (n^3)	1, 8, 27, 64, 125...
Fibonacci Sequence	Each number is the sum of the two numbers before it	0, 1, 1, 2, 3, 5, 8, 13, 21...
Triangular Sequence	Each number adds what would be another row to a triangle of dots $x_n = n(n+1)/2$	. . . . A numerical example of a triangular sequence: 1, 3, 6, 10, 15, 21, 28, 36...

Shape Patterns

Patterns in shapes may involve shape, size, color, rotation, or other physical attributes of the shapes used to create a recognizable pattern. Students will be expected to articulate, predict, and create shape patterns.

Two common types of shape patterns are patterns of repetition and patterns of symmetry.

Patterns of repetition involve the repetition of elements in a predictable sequence.

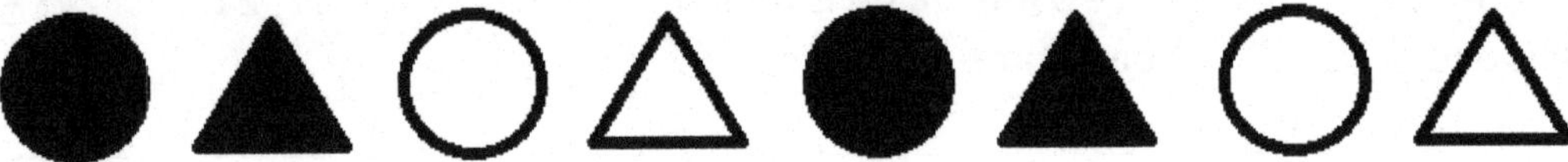

Patterns of symmetry have a line of symmetry which creates a mirror image within the pattern.

A **linear function** is one whose graph is a straight line.

The equation of a line is commonly written in what is called **slope-intercept form**: ***y* = *mx* + *b*,** where *x* and *y* are the coordinates of any point on the line, *m* is the slope of the line, and *b* is the y-intercept (the value of *y* where the line crosses the y-axis.

The slope of a line can be found using any two points on the line with the **slope formula:** $m = \frac{y_2 - y_1}{x_2 - x_1}$

Example: Find the equation of the line shown on the graph below.

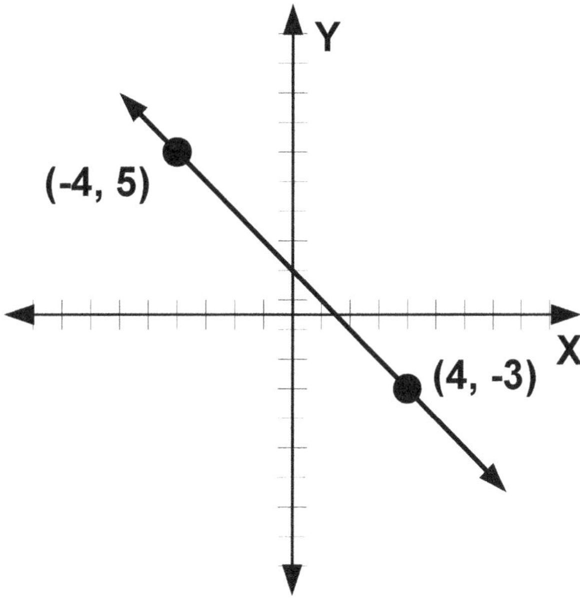

To generate the equation of the line, you need to know the slope *(m)* and the y- intercept (*b*). The y-intercept in this case is 2, since the line crosses the y-axis at (0,2).

Use the slope formula to find the slope of the line:

$m = \frac{y_2 - y_1}{x_2 - x_1} = \frac{-3-5}{4-(-4)} = \frac{-8}{8} = -1$

Insert these values into the slope-intercept form to get the equation of the line.

$y = mx + b$

$y = -x + 2$

Geometry and Measurement

Geometry is the branch of mathematics concerned with the study of points, lines, shapes, and space. At the elementary level, students learn basic geometric concepts and properties, and how to use geometric concepts to solve mathematical and real-world problems. Students also learn to measure and interpret data using different systems and forms of representation. This content accounts for 18% of the Mathematics subtest.

Topics Addressed:

1. Concepts of Measurement
2. Concepts of Geometry

Concepts of Measurement

Students will learn to understand measurement concepts using different sets of units. The three main types of units students will encounter are nonstandard, customary, and metric units.

Nonstandard Measurement

Nonstandard measurement is how elementary students first learn to measure. The use of nonstandard units often involves measuring using small objects such as paper clips.

Customary Measurement

Customary measurement is the primary system of measurement used in the United States. There are customary units to measure length, weight, volume, temperature, and time.

Length is measured in inches, feet, yards, and miles using measuring tools such as rulers and measuring tapes.

- 12 inches (in. or ") = 1 foot (ft. or ')
- 36 inches = 3 feet = 1 yard (yd.)
- 5,280 feet = 1,760 yards = 1 mile (mi.)

Weight is measured in ounces, pounds, and tons using a scale.

- 16 ounces (oz.) = 1 pound (lb.)
- 1,000 pounds = 1 ton (T.)

Volume is measured in fluid ounces, cups, pints, quarts, and gallons using a measuring cup, beaker, or other marked container for holding liquid.

- 8 fluid ounces (fl. oz.) = 1 cup (c.)
- 16 fluid ounces = 2 cups = 1 pint (pt.)

- 4 cups = 2 pints = 1 quart (qt.)
- 8 pints = 4 quarts = 1 gallon (gal.)

Temperature is measured in degrees Fahrenheit (ºF) using a thermometer.

Time is measured in seconds, minutes, and hours using a clock.

- 60 seconds (sec.) = 1 minute (min.)
- 60 minutes = 1 hour (hr.)

Metric Measurement

The metric system of measurement is used in most of the world. It is based on units that are multiples of ten. No matter what is being measured, the units have prefixes which tell you the size of the unit relative to the others of its type.

The basic unit for each form of measurement is:

- Length- meter
- Mass- gram
- Volume- liter

Adding one of the prefixes in the chart below changes the value.

Kilo-	Hecto-	Deka-	Unit	Deci-	Centi-	Milli-
.001	.01	.1	1	10	100	1000

For example, this means that 1 gram is equal to 1000 milligrams. To convert between units in the metric system, simply use this chart to determine how many places to move the decimal.

The metric system has two scales for measuring temperature—Celsius (ºC) and Kelvin (K).

Points

A point is an exact location on a plane surface.

. P

On a coordinate plane, a point is identified by a set of coordinates, giving the x and y values of the point's location on the coordinate plane.

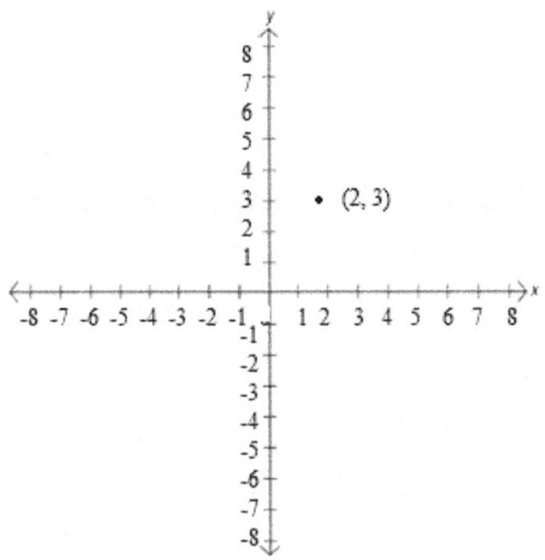

Lines, Line Segments, and Rays

A line is an object that is straight, thin, and infinitely long. It has arrows on both ends to show that it goes on forever in both directions.

l

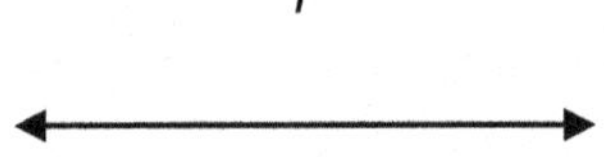

Two special types of lines are parallel lines and perpendicular lines. Parallel lines are always equally spaced so that they never intersect each other.

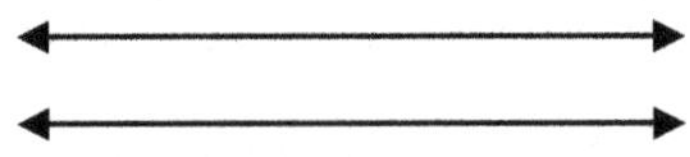

Perpendicular lines intersect at a 90º angle.

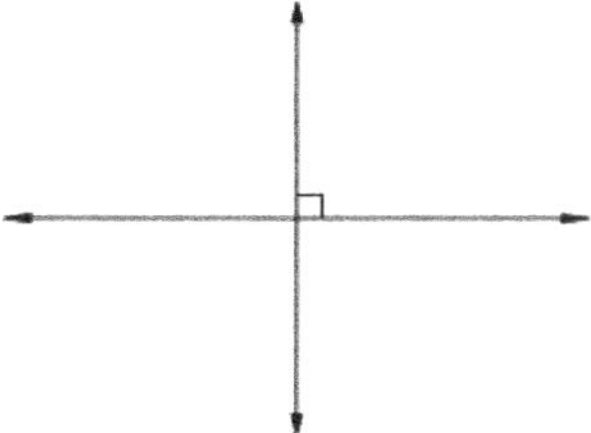

A **line segment** is a portion of a line that has two endpoints, which give it a definite length.

A **ray** has only one endpoint and is infinite in the other direction.

Angles

An **angle** is the space formed by two rays that meet at a common endpoint. Angles are measured in degrees.

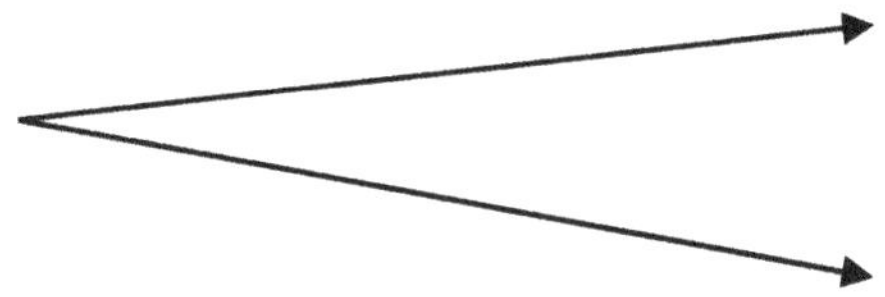

Angle Type	Definition	Example
Acute	The angle measures less than 90º	
Right	The angle measures exactly 90º	
Obtuse	The angle measures between 90º and 180º	
Straight	The angle measures exactly 180º	
Reflex	The angle measures greater than 180º	

Angles can also be described by their relationships to one another.

Complimentary angles are those whose measures add up to 90º.

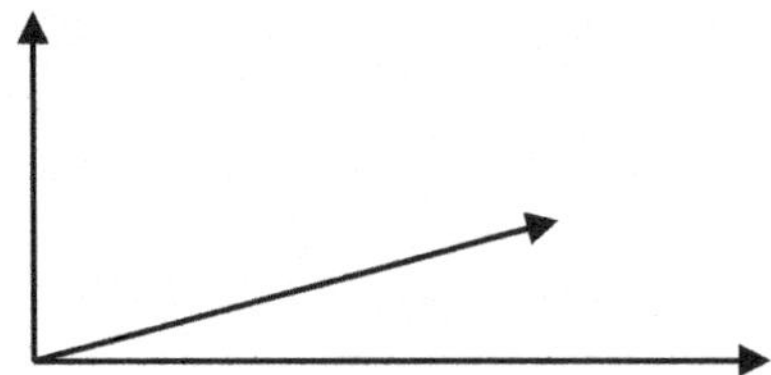

Supplementary angles are those whose measures add up to 180º.

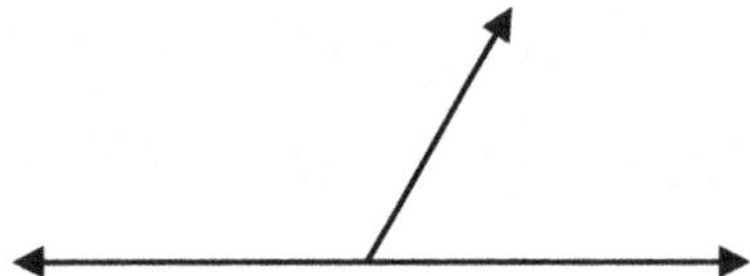

Two-Dimensional Shapes

A two-dimensional closed figure can be classified either as a polygon or a non-polygon. A **polygon** is a closed two-dimensional figure whose sides are all straight, non-overlapping line segments. A polygon is said to be **regular** if all of its sides and angles are equal and irregular if they are not. **Non-polygons** do not have sides that are all straight line segments and include such shapes as ellipses and circles. Polygons can be classified by the number of sides they have.

Name	Number of Sides
Triangle	3
Quadrilateral	4
Pentagon	5
Hexagon	6
Heptagon	7
Octagon	8
Nonagon	9
Decagon	10

Some of these categories of polygons can also be further broken down into subcategories. The most common ones elementary students will encounter are triangles and quadrilaterals. Triangles can be classified either by the types of angles they have or the length of their sides.

Triangles Classified by Angles		
Type of Triangles	**Description**	**Example**
Acute	All three angles are acute (measure less than 90º)	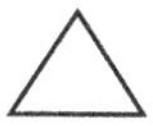
Right	One angle is right (measures exactly 90º)	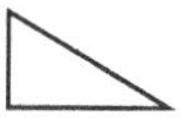
Obtuse	One angle is obtuse (measures between 90º and 180º)	

Triangles Classified by Sides		
Type of Triangles	**Description**	**Example**
Equilateral	All three sides are equal in length	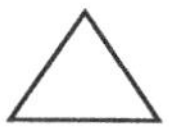
Isosceles	Two sides are equal in length	
Scalene	No sides are equal in length	

Quadrilaterals can be divided into several subcategories based on characteristics such as angles, parallelism, and side length.

Quadrilateral- *four sides*	
Trapezoid- *one pair of parallel sides*	**Parallelogram**- *two pairs of equal parallel sides*

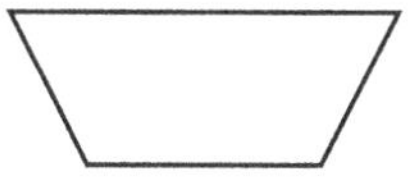

Rectangle- *four right angles* 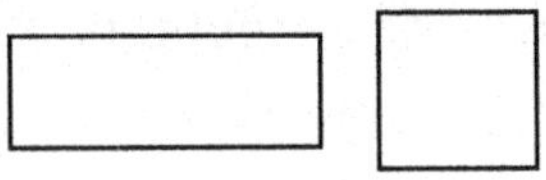	**Rhombus--** *four equal sides* 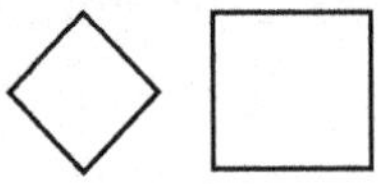
Square - *four right angles and four equal sides*	

Three-Dimensional Shapes

A three-dimensional shape is a solid figure. Three-dimensional shapes are classified by their faces (the shape of each side and how many there are), their edges (where two face meet), and their vertices (points). There are several categories of solid figures, some of which are listed in the following chart:

Shape	Description	Example
Sphere	Round three-dimensional figure, like a ball	
Pyramid	Triangular of square base, with all other sides triangular that come together at a single point	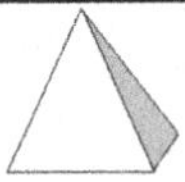
Rectangular prism	Six rectangular faces	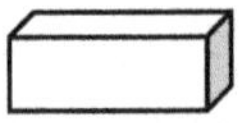
Cylinder	Two circular bases	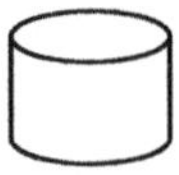
Cone	One circular base	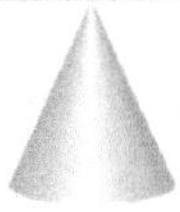
Cube	Six square faces	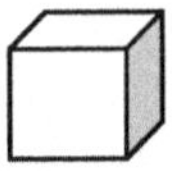

Geometric Models and Nets

A **geometric model** can be constructed to show the shape of an object in geometric terms.

Geometric nets are two-dimensional figures that represent the faces of a three-dimensional shape. It's as if the three-dimensional figure has been cut apart along the edges and made to lay flat. Only certain three-dimensional figures can be made into geometric nets. Two of the most common examples are cubes and tetrahedrons (pyramids with a triangular base).

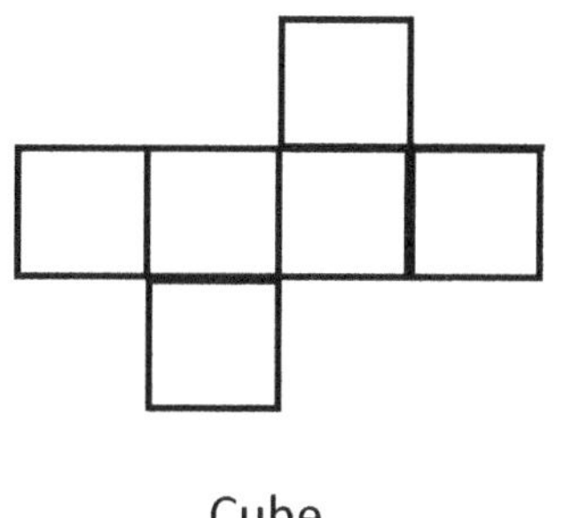

Cube

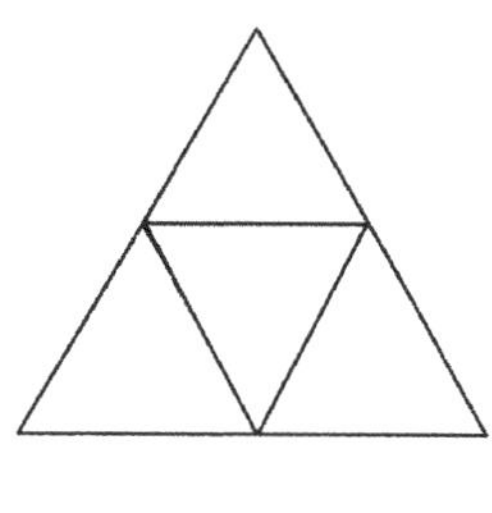

Tetrahedron

Comparing Geometric Figures

Geometric figures can be compared using congruence and similarity.

Two figures are said to be **congruent** if they are exactly the same shape and size. The figures may be rotated, but the size and shape remain the same.

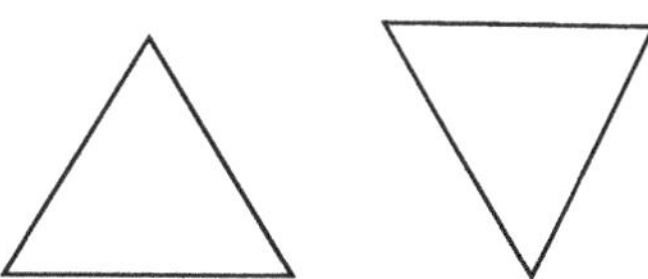

Two figures are said to be **similar** if they are the same shape (having the same angles and proportions) but different sizes.

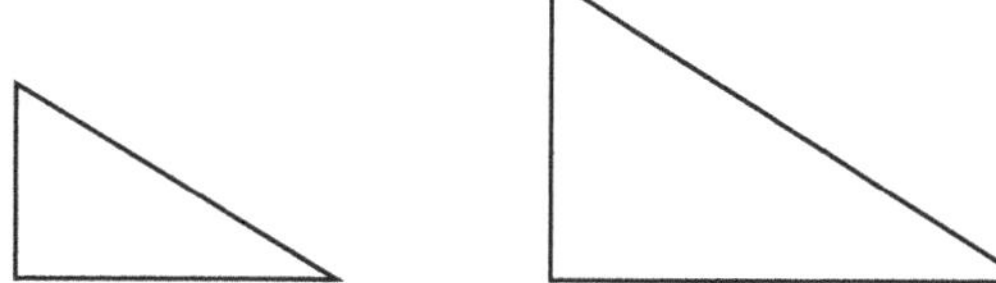

Symmetry

Symmetry creates a mirror image. A line of symmetry that passes through a shape divides the shape into two congruent halves such that the pieces are mirror images of one another. A shape can have no, one, or multiple lines of symmetry.

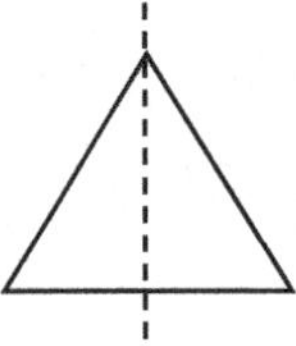

Measurements of Two-Dimensional Figures

The measure of the distance around a polygon is called the **perimeter**. The perimeter is found by adding up the lengths of all of the sides of a figure.

The distance around the outside of a circle is called the **circumference.** The circumference is found with the formula $C = \pi d$ or $C = 2\pi r$ where r is the radius and d is the diameter.

The measure of the space inside a two-dimensional figure is called the **area**.

Common Area Formulas	
Triangle	$A = \frac{1}{2} bh$
Parallelogram	$A = bh$
Rectangle	$A = lw$
Square	$A = s^2$
Circle	$A = \pi r^2$

Measurements of Three-Dimensional Figures

The measure of the **surface area** of a prism is found by adding up the areas of each of the faces. The measure of the space inside a three-dimensional object (its capacity) is called **volume**.

- Volume of a prism:

  $V = bh$ where b is the area of the base of the prism

- Volume of a pyramid or cone:

  V = $\frac{1}{3}bh$ where b is the area of the base of the object

- Volume of a sphere:

  V = $\frac{4}{3}\pi r^3$

Transformations

Transformations are a way of manipulating geometric figures by changing their positions on a coordinate plane. There are three basic types of transformations.

Name of Transformation	Description	Example
Reflection (Flip)	The transformed shape is a mirror image of the original	
Rotation (Turn)	The shape is turned on a point	
Translation (Slide)	The shape is shifted to another area on the plane but maintains its original orientation	

Coordinate Graphing

Coordinate graphing is a visual method of showing the relationships between numbers. Points, lines, geometric figures, equations, inequalities, and functions can all be represented using a coordinate graphing system.

The graphing space is called a **coordinate plane**. It consists of a grid created by a horizontal (x) axis and a vertical (y) axis.

The point where the two axes intersect is called the origin and has coordinates of (0,0). Every other point on the plane is given **coordinates** (locations) based on its distance from the origin. A point's location in reference to the x-axis is its x-coordinate and its location in reference to the y-axis is its y-coordinate. Coordinates are always listed in parenthesis in the format (x,y) and are called an **ordered pair**.

The graph below shows how points are given coordinates and located on a coordinate plane.

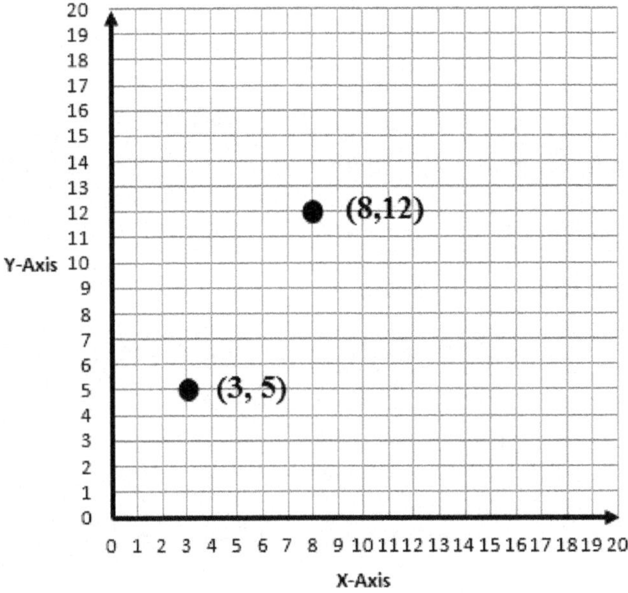

Coordinate grids can show both positive and negative values. Since the axes extend infinitely in each direction, any pair of numbers can be graphed. When the axes are extended in all directions, it creates a grid with four quadrants. The most commonly used quadrant is the first quadrant as seen above. The four quadrants together look like this:

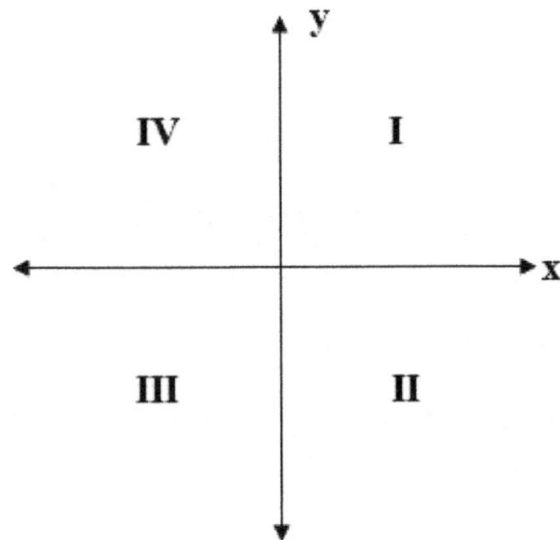

Points located in these quadrants have positive or negative coordinate values as follows:

- Quadrant I: (positive, positive)
- Quadrant II: (positive, negative)
- Quadrant III: (negative, negative)
- Quadrant IV: (negative, positive)

Coordinate planes are also commonly used to graph lines and other equations. See "Linear Functions and Equations" for the equations used to graph lines and to find slopes on a coordinate plane.

Statistics and Probability

This section covers the use of descriptive statistics for data analysis, as well as the fundamental concepts of probability. This content accounts for 9% of the Mathematics subtest.

Topics Addressed:

1. Descriptive Statistics
2. Probability

Descriptive Statistics

Descriptive statistics are used to explain patterns and relationships among sets of data. The basic types of descriptive statistics include mean, median, mode, range, and frequency distribution.

Mean

Mean is another word for average. To find the mean of a set of numbers, add the numbers together and divide the sum by how many numbers there are.

Example:

Find the mean of the following set: (12, 15, 18, 20, 21)

$$\frac{12+15+18+20+21}{5} = \frac{86}{5} = 17.2$$

Absolute Deviation

Absolute deviation is a measure of how far a value in a set is from the mean of the set. For example, in the set used in the example for mean above, the mean was 17.2. The absolute deviation of each term in the set is the distance from that term to 17.2. So the absolute deviation of 12 is 5.2; the absolute deviation of 15 is 2.2; the absolute deviation of 18 is 0.8; etc.

Median

The median of a set of numbers is the number that is in the middle of the set when they are arranged in numerical order. If there are an even number of digits, the median is found by taking the average of the two numbers that are in the center (add them and divide by 2).

Example 1: *Find the median of the following set: (34, 25, 82, 11, 47)*

In order, the set would read 11, 25, 34, 47, 82.

The number in the middle (the median) is 34.

Example 2: *Find the median of the following set: (47, 23, 24, 89, 23, 43)*

In order, the set would read 23, 23, 24, 43, 47, 89.

In the middle are 24 and 43. Take their average to find the median.

$$\frac{24+43}{2} = \frac{67}{2} = 33.5$$

Mode

The mode is the number in a set that appears the most frequently. A set can have one mode, more than one mode, or no mode.

Example: *Find the mode of the following set: (34, 52, 34, 58, 31, 19)*

The number that appears most frequently is 34. 34 is the mode.

Range

The **range** of a set describes the span between the numbers. The range is calculated by subtracting the lowest value in the set from the highest.

Example: *Find the range of the following set: (2, 59, 27)*

The highest number in the set is 59. The lowest number is 2.

59 – 2 = 57

The range is 57.

Frequency Distribution

Frequency distribution is a representation of how many times the same event or piece of data occurs. Frequency distribution is often displayed in a table.

Example: *The scores on a recent math test were 100, 98, 95, 98, 86, 84, 80, 84, 75, 68, 80, 84, and 77. Create a table to show the frequency distribution of the scores.*

Score	Frequency
100	1
98	2
95	1
86	1
84	3
80	2
77	1
75	1
68	1

Probability is the likelihood of an event occurring. Probability is expressed as a quantifiable relationship between favorable outcomes and possible outcomes. It can be written as a ratio, fraction, decimal, or percent.

A **favorable outcome** is an event someone wants to happen. **Possible outcomes** are all of the events that could happen in a given situation.

Simple probability (P) is the ratio of favorable outcomes (O_f) to possible outcomes (O_p).

$$P_{event} = \frac{O_f}{O_p}$$

Example 1: *What is the probability of a coin toss landing on heads?*

When flipping a coin, there are two possible outcomes—heads or tails. The probability of getting heads is 1/2.

Example 2: *What is the probability of rolling a 5 on a die?*

When rolling a standard six-sided die, there are six possible outcomes. Rolling a 5 (the favorable outcome) is one of those possibilities. The probability of rolling a 5 is therefore 1/6.

Example 3: *Using a spinner with equal segments numbered 1-10, what is the probability of a spin landing on an even number?*

In this case, there are ten possible outcomes—landing on each of the ten segments. The favorable outcome is landing on an even number. In the set of numbers 1-10, there are five even numbers (2, 4, 6, 8, and 10). Any one of these would be a favorable outcome. The probability of landing on a even number is therefore 5/10, which reduces to 1/2.

The Fundamental Counting Principle

The **fundamental counting principle** states that if there are *m* ways to for one thing to happen and *n* ways for another thing to happen, then there are *m* x *n* ways for both to happen.

> Example:
> *If you have 5 shirts and 3 pairs of pants, how many different outfits could you make?*
>
> 5 x 3 = 15 outfits

These types of problems can also be solved using a visual aid called a **tree diagram**. A tree diagram lists all of the possible combinations of two events. The tree diagram for the example scenario above would look like this:

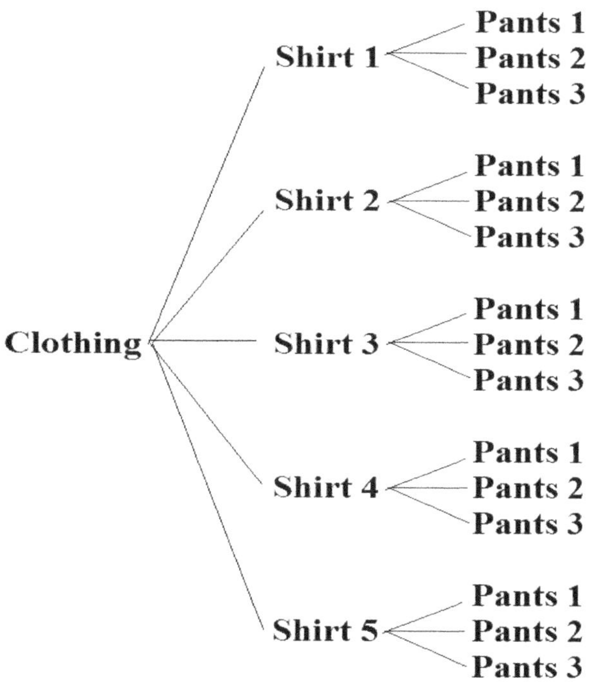

Counting all of the right-most possibilities (those farthest from the "trunk" of the tree) gives the total number of possibilities. In this case, the total is twelve possible outcomes.

Combinations

A **combination** involves choosing items (r) out of a group (n) in a situation where the order does not matter and there is no repetition.

The formula for a combination is:

$$_nC_r = \frac{n!}{(n-r)!r!}$$

This formula involves the use of **factorials**, represented by the exclamation point (!). A factorial is the product of a number and all of the counting numbers below it.

For example, 4! = 4 x 3 x 2 x 1 = 24

Example: *How many different groups of 3 students can be made from a class of 21?*

$$_nC_r = \frac{n!}{(n-r)!r!}$$

$$_{21}C_3 = \frac{21!}{(21-3)!3!}$$

$$_{21}C_3 = \frac{51090942171709440000}{18!3!}$$

$$_{21}C_3 = \frac{51090942171709440000}{(6402373705728000)(6)}$$

$$_{21}C_3 = \frac{51090942171709440000}{38414242234368000}$$

$$_{21}C_3 = 1{,}330$$

There are 1,330 possible groups.

Permutations

Permutations involve selecting items (*r*) out of a group (*n*) wherein the order *does* matter and there is no repetition. These problems involve arranging items in a certain order.

The formula for a permutation is:

$$_nP_r = \frac{n!}{(n-r)!}$$

Example: *How many different three-digit numbers can be made using only the digits 1, 3, 5, and 7?*

There are 4 digits to choose from and 3 are being selected.

$_nP_r = \frac{n!}{(n-r)!}$

$_4P_3 = \frac{4!}{(4-3)!}$

$_4P_3 = \frac{24}{1}$

$_4P_3 = 24$

There are 24 possible three-digit numbers.

Open-Response Questions:

Integration of Knowledge and Understanding

10% of your overall score on each subtest comes from a single open-response question. You will be expected to produce a 1-2 page written response to a prompt.

Multi-Subject Subtest:

"Prepare an organized, developed analysis on a topic related to History and Social Science or to Science and Technology/Engineering." (from the MTEL Test Objectives)

You will be given a multi-part question in one of these content areas (History and Social Science or Science and Technology/Engineering; *not* Language Arts) that will require you to go beyond stating facts and show that you can analyze processes.

Mathematics Subtest:

"Apply mathematical knowledge and reasoning to communicate multiple solutions in detail to a problem involving two or more of the following subareas: Numbers and Operations, Functions and Algebra, Geometry and Measurement, and Statistics and Probability." (from the MTEL Test Objectives)

These questions will test your mathematical content knowledge by asking you to analyze a problem, posit one or more approaches to solving the problem, and articulate your reasoning.

For example, a common type of prompt is one that provides you with a mathematical problem and a student response to that problem and asks you to make corrections to the student's response, explain any errors, propose an alternative method of solving, and explain your reasoning process.

Scoring:

You will be graded on the following:

1. Purpose: Did you achieve the purpose of the assignment?
2. Subject Knowledge: Does your response indicate a thorough grasp of the subject matter and show appropriate, accurate applications of concepts?
3. Support: Did you provide relevant evidence to support your reasoning?
4. Rationale: How well-reasoned and explained is your argument?

Responses will be scored from 1-4 according to the following scale:

Score	Score Description
4	**The "4" response reflects a thorough knowledge and understanding of the subject matter.** • The purpose of the assignment is fully achieved. • There is substantial, accurate, and appropriate application of subject matter knowledge. • The supporting evidence is sound; there are high-quality, relevant examples. • The response reflects an ably reasoned, comprehensive understanding of the topic.
3	**The "3" response reflects an adequate knowledge and understanding of the subject matter.** • The purpose of the assignment is largely achieved. • There is a generally accurate and appropriate application of subject matter knowledge. • The supporting evidence is adequate; there are some acceptable, relevant examples. • The response reflects an adequately reasoned understanding of the topic.
2	**The "2" response reflects a limited knowledge and understanding of the subject matter.** • The purpose of the assignment is partially achieved. • There is a limited, possibly inaccurate or inappropriate, application of subject matter knowledge. • The supporting evidence is limited; there are few relevant examples. • The response reflects a limited, poorly reasoned understanding of the topic.
1	**The "1" response reflects a weak knowledge and understanding of the subject matter.** • The purpose of the assignment is not achieved. • There is little or no appropriate or accurate application of subject matter knowledge. • The supporting evidence, if present, is weak; there are few or no relevant examples.

	• The response reflects little or no reasoning about or understanding of the topic.
U	The response is unrelated to the assigned topic, illegible, primarily in a language other than English, not of sufficient length to score, or merely a repetition of the assignment.
B	There is no response to the assignment.

Practice Examination

Multi-Subject Subtest

1. Which type of rock is formed by the cooling of magma?

A. Sedimentary
B. Igneous
C. Metamorphic
D. Cretaceous

2. The overall charge of the nucleus of an atom is

A. negative
B. positive
C. neutral
D. dependent on the element

3. Which of the following is an example of hyperbole?

A. She was as clever as a fox.
B. I've been waiting in this line forever.
C. The bright blue balloon floated away.
D. It was a real Cinderella story.

Question 4 refers to the following passage:

Whose woods these are I think I know.
His house is in the village, though;
He will not see me stopping here
To watch his woods fill up with snow.

My little horse must think it queer
To stop without a farmhouse near
Between the woods and frozen lake
The darkest evening of the year.

He gives his harness bells a shake
To ask if there is some mistake.
The only other sound's the sweep
Of easy wind and downy flake.

The woods are lovely, dark, and deep,
But I have promises to keep,
And miles to go before I sleep,
And miles to go before I sleep.
—Robert Frost

4. According to the narrator, why does he not stay to watch the snow longer?

A. His horse is anxious.
B. He is afraid the homeowner will see him.
C. He is afraid of the dark.
D. He has somewhere else he needs to be.

5. Latin America is an example of a

A. continent
B. country
C. biome
D. region

6. Which part of a plant is responsible for reproduction?

A. Stem
B. Roots
C. Leaves
D. Flower

7. A question mark is most likely to be used in which type of sentence?

A. Declarative
B. Interrogative
C. Imperative
D. Exclamatory

8. In order to be considered a sentence, a group of words must at least contain

A. a noun and a verb
B. a noun and a conjunction
C. a verb and a conjunction
D. a noun and an adverb

9. The Gadsden Purchase, the Mexican Cession, and the Louisiana Purchase were part of the United States'

A. belief in Manifest Destiny
B. New Deal programs
C. 20th century imperialism
D. Cold War era policy

10. The human body system responsible for the transport of blood is the

A. respiratory system
B. musculoskeletal system
C. circulatory system
D. nervous system

11. Which of the following requires chemical bonding of its different component parts?

A. Mixture
B. Element
C. Solution
D. Compound

12. The evolution of the way in which scientists throughout have understood the arrangement of the solar system demonstrates which component of the nature of science?

A. Durability
B. Replication
C. Tentativeness
D. Inflexibility

13. Natural selection contributes to biological evolution by

A. ensuring that mutations favorable for survival are passed down through reproduction
B. eliminating all mutations from the gene pool
C. providing a means for weaker organisms to survive and reproduce
D. ensuring that only dominant traits can be genetically inherited

14. Which of these types of water movement in the water cycle does NOT involve a phase change?

A. Melting
B. Surface run-off
C. Transpiration
D. Evaporation

Question 15 refers to the following passage:

JULIET: (to Romeo) Good night, good night! parting is such
sweet sorrow,
That I shall say good night till it be morrow.
-*Romeo and Juliet* by William Shakespeare (Act 2, Scene 2)

15. The passage above is an example of

A. monologue
B. soliloquy
C. dialogue
D. prose

16. Which simple machine would be most useful for moving an object across a long horizontal distance?

A. Pulley
B. Lever
C. Wedge
D. Wheel and axle

17. Which of these groups were the last to receive suffrage nationwide in the United States?

A. Women
B. African-American males
C. Those between the ages of 18 and 20
D. White males

18. In an experiment to see the effects of three different types of plant food on the growth of a plant, the control group

A. is the plant given the most successful type of plant food
B. is a plant that is given less water than the other plants
C. is a dependent variable
D. is a plant that receives no plant food, but all other conditions are the same as the other plants

19. Identify the error in the following sentences: "Maria moved to New York City last month. She lived in Brooklyn where she works in a café."

A. Subject-verb agreement
B. Tense agreement
C. Ambiguous antecedent
D. Punctuation

20. "She was as tall as a giraffe" is an example of a(n)

A. onomatopoeia
B. simile
C. metaphor
D. foil

21. Which of these civilizations was the first to use a civil service exam?

A. India
B. China
C. Mesopotamia
D. Egypt

22. Which of the following types of writing should NOT include the author's personal opinion?

A. Journaling
B. Expository writing
C. Poetry
D. Persuasive writing

Questions 23-24 refer to the following passage:

"Tom appeared on the sidewalk with a bucket of whitewash and a long-handled brush. He surveyed the fence, and all gladness left him and a deep melancholy settled down upon his spirit. Thirty yards of board fence nine feet high. Life to him seemed hollow, and existence but a burden. Sighing, he dipped his brush and passed it along the topmost plank; repeated the operation; did it again; compared the insignificant whitewashed streak with the far-reaching continent of unwhitewashed fence, and sat down on a tree-box discouraged."

-From *The Adventures of Tom Sawyer* by Mark Twain

23. The comparison of the "insignificant whitewashed streak" to the "far-reaching continent of unwhitewashed fence" is used to

A. provide a precise measurement of the painted area
B. demonstrate how hard Tom had been working
C. emphasize the perceived enormity of Tom's task
D. portray Tom as unintelligent

24. In this passage, Tom appears to be

A. dedicated
B. reluctant
C. motivated
D. inventive

25. When using a Bunsen burner, students should NOT

A. turn the burner to a high flame to produce more heat
B. leave a burner unattended
C. hold metal objects over the flame without using gloves
D. All of the above

26. Which of these is ALWAYS true of an object in equilibrium?

A. It is at rest.
B. It is in motion.
C. The resultant of all forces acting on the object is zero.
D. It is subject only to normal force.

27. The most powerful unifying force in medieval Europe was

A. the Roman Catholic Church
B. the Holy Roman Emperor
C. the British navy
D. the Silk Road

28. Which of the following is NOT a characteristic of all living things?

A. Made of cells
B. Have definite life spans
C. Use energy
D. Sexual reproduction

29. Which of these was NOT a direct result of the Industrial Revolution in the United States?

A. The population became more urbanized.
B. Manufactured goods became more widely available and less expensive.
C. Big businesses were subject to strict government regulations.
D. Factories employed many immigrants for low wages.

Question 30 refers to the following passage:

"The history of the present King of Great Britain is a history of repeated injuries and usurpations, all having in direct object the establishment of an absolute tyranny over these States...

In every stage of these oppressions, we have petitioned for redress in the most humble terms: Our repeated petitions have been answered only by repeated injury. A prince whose character is thus marked by every act which may define a tyrant, is unfit to be the ruler of a free people...

We, therefore, the Representatives of the united States of America, in General Congress, Assembled, appealing to the Supreme Judge of the world for the rectitude of our intentions, do, in the name, and by authority of the good people of these Colonies, solemnly publish and declare, that these United Colonies are, and of right ought to be free and independent states; that they are absolved from all allegiance to the British Crown, and that all political connection between them and the State of Great Britain, is and ought to be totally dissolved."

–Second Continental Congress, 1776

30. The original intended audience of this document was

A. the British monarch
B. the government of the United States
C. future generations of Americans
D. Loyalists

31. The last half of the twentieth century in the United States was most shaped by

A. disputes over the issue of slavery
B. competition with the Soviet Union
C. the desire for territorial expansion
D. military conflict with Germany

32. Which of these terms refers to the limited nature of resources which drives economics?

A. Surplus
B. Scarcity
C. Demand
D. Tariff

33. Which of the following would be the best topic sentence for a persuasive essay?

A. World War II was a fight between the Axis and the Allies.
B. World War II took place between 1939 and 1945.
C. The use of the atomic bomb during World War II was not justified.
D. New technologies were used in World War II.

34. Meteorites are found

A. within the Earth's atmosphere
B. in the asteroid belt
C. near the sun
D. nowhere in this solar system

35. The idea that an object in motion will stay in motion unless acted upon by an outside force is known as

A. sublimation
B. velocity
C. inertia
D. friction

36. The esophagus is part of which human body system?

A. Respiratory system
B. Digestive system
C. Nervous system
D. Reproductive system

37. The purpose of a(n) _______________ is to carry out the day-to-day functions of a government.

A. legislature
B. bureaucracy
C. judicial system
D. executive

38. Which of these does NOT contain meter?

A. Blank verse
B. Limerick
C. Free verse
D. Sonnet

39. A paleontologist is most likely to study

A. the skeletal remains of a dinosaur
B. pottery left by an ancient civilization
C. constellations
D. weather patterns

40. "Pretty ugly" is an example of a(n)

A. onomatopoeia
B. oxymoron
C. allusion
D. hyperbole

41. Which of the following would be the best thesis statement for a persuasive essay on World War II?

A. World War II was a fight between the Axis and the Allies.
B. World War II took place between 1939 and 1945.
C. The use of the atomic bomb during World War II was not justified.
D. New technologies were used in World War II.

42. One result of the Neolithic Revolution was

A. a reliance on hunting and gathering for food
B. the adoption of a nomadic lifestyle
C. the development of permanent settlements
D. a decrease in trade between people groups

43. In the writing process, which step follows revising?

A. Publishing
B. Creating a rough draft
C. Editing
D. Prewriting

44. Humans, more than any other species,

A. are dependent on their environment
B. alter their environment
C. don't use the resources from the natural environment
D. are unaffected by environmental factors

45. A country that exports more than it imports is said to have

A. a market economy
B. inflation
C. a favorable balance of trade
D. a shortage of consumer goods

46. A topographic map would be most useful for

A. calculating the population density of New York City
B. finding the elevation of Beijing
C. seeing how the borders of Poland have changed over time
D. identifying the major agricultural products of France

47. In a laissez-faire system, economics are driven by

A. government planning
B. collective decision-making
C. market forces
D. regulatory action

48. "Manuscript," "transcription," and "descriptive" share a common

A. prefix
B. suffix
C. end rhyme
D. root word

49. Which of these words does NOT contain an affix?

A. Bicycle
B. Largest
C. Start
D. Prediction

50. "Teacher picked up book off of floor." This sentence is missing

A. articles
B. verbs
C. prepositions
D. nouns

51. The desire to satisfy curiosity and to find practical applications of scientific understandings are

A. integrated process skills of engineering
B. two of the primary motivations for scientific inquiry
C. stages in the experiential learning process
D. elements of the tentativeness of scientific knowledge

52. Two of the main causes of the Civil War were

A. slavery and states' rights
B. boundary disputes and states' rights
C. slavery and taxation
D. taxation and boundary disputes

53. The amount of solar radiation a location receives is influenced by

A. the longitude of the location
B. the position of the Moon
C. the tilt of the Earth
D. Plate tectonics

54. Aqueducts were an important feature in the architecture of

A. the Indus Valley Civilization
B. Egypt
C. Rome
D. Sumer

55. Changing "cat" to "bat" is an example of

A. phoneme segmentation
B. phoneme substitution
C. phoneme identification
D. phoneme blending

DIRECTIONS FOR THE OPEN-RESPONSE ITEM ASSIGNMENT

This section of the test consists of an open-response item assignment that appears on the following page. You will be asked to prepare a written response of approximately 150–300 words, or 1–2 pages, for the assignment. You should use your time to plan, write, review, and edit your response for the assignment.

Read the topic and directions for the assignment carefully before you begin to work. Think about how you will organize your response.

As a whole, your response to the assignment must demonstrate an understanding of the knowledge of the field. In your response to the assignment, you are expected to demonstrate the depth of your understanding of the subject area by applying your knowledge rather than by merely reciting factual information.

Your response to the assignment will be evaluated based on the following criteria.

- PURPOSE: the extent to which the response achieves the purpose of the assignment
- SUBJECT KNOWLEDGE: appropriateness and accuracy in the application of subject knowledge
- SUPPORT: quality and relevance of supporting evidence
- RATIONALE: soundness of argument and degree of understanding of the subject area

The open-response item assignment is intended to assess subject knowledge. Your response must be communicated clearly enough to permit valid judgment of the evaluation criteria by scorers. Your response should be written for an audience of educators in this field. The final version of your response should conform to the conventions of edited American English. Your response should be your original work, written in your own words, and not copied or paraphrased from some other work.

Be sure to write about the assigned topic. Please write legibly. You may not use any reference materials during the test. Remember to review your work and make any changes you think will improve your response.

Write or print your response in the space provided following the assignment.

OPEN RESPONSE ITEM ASSIGNMENT

Use the information below to complete the exercise that follows.

In the sixteenth century, Europe underwent a religious movement known as the Protestant Reformation, in which various reformers broke away from the Roman Catholic Church to start new denominations.

Using your knowledge of this period in history:

- explain how and why the Protestant Reformation began
- explain the impact of technology on the Protestant Reformation
- describe two effects of the Protestant Reformation

Mathematics Subtest

1. **Using a spinner with equal segments numbered 1-6, what is the probability of a spin landing on an even number?**
   A. 1/6
   B. 1/3
   C. 5/6
   D. 1/2

2. **Which of these fractions is equal to 0.875?**
   A. 9/10
   B. 7/8
   C. 6/7
   D. 11/12

3. **Which of these units is NOT used to measure liquid volume?**
   A. pints
   B. milliliters
   C. grams
   D. cups

4. **There were 25 questions on a spelling test. If Kristen got 21 of them correct, what was her score expressed as a percentage?**
   A. 21%
   B. 0.84
   C. 0.96
   D. 0.74

5. **To convert a mixed number to an improper fraction, ____________ the denominator by the whole number and ______________ the numerator.**
   A. multiply, add
   B. divide, add
   C. add, multiply
   D. add, divide

6. x^0=

A. x
B. -x
C. 1
D. 0

7. Which of the following is does NOT describe the number 98?

A. Real
B. Rational
C. Prime
D. Composite

8. A take-apart problem may contain any of the following EXCEPT

A. an unknown subtrahend
B. an unknown quotient
C. an unknown minuend
D. an unknown difference

9. Which of the following best illustrates the commutative property?

A. 4 + 2 = 2 + 4
B. (2 + 4) + 3 = 2 + (4 + 3)
C. 2(4 + 3) = (2 * 4) + (2 * 3)
D. 4 – 2 = 2 – 4

10. Which of these is NOT equivalent to 80 cm?

A. 0.8 m
B. 0.008 km
C. 800 mm
D. 80.0 cm

11. Which of these is considered an integer?

A. .5
B. -5
C. 1/5
D. 1.5

12. Solve for x. $-4x < 16$

A. $x > -4$

B. $x < -4$

C. $x < 4$

D. $x > 4$

13. An angle that measures 100° is considered

A. acute

B. obtuse

C. straight

D. right

14. If a car travels at 55 mph, how far will the car travel in 2 hours and 30 minutes?

A. 140 miles

B. 175 miles

C. 12,650 miles

D. 137.5 miles

15. When presented with two fractions with the same numerator and different denominators, a student would need to find a common denominator in order to

A. multiply the fractions

B. divide the fractions

C. compare the fractions

D. add the fractions

16. Tiling can be used to find the area of a

A. rectangle

B. circle

C. triangle

D. oval

17. The product of two numbers is 12. The difference of these numbers is 4. What is the larger of the two numbers?

A. 4
B. 6
C. 12
D. 3

18. The mean of a set is 15.6. The lowest value in the set is 10.2. The highest value in the set is 21.8. What is the absolute deviation of the highest value in the set?

A. 6.2
B. 11.6
C. 5.4
D. 2.6

19. On a recent test, five friends had scores of 88, 92, 76, 94, and 80. What was their median score?

A. 86
B. 88
C. 94
D. 90

20. The area of a right triangle whose sides measure 3 cm, 5 cm, and 4 cm is

A. 6
B. 7.5
C. 10
D. 12

21. A store buys t-shirts from the manufacturer in cases of 25 for $50. They sell the shirts for a price of $8 each. How much of a profit will the store make on the sale of 80 shirts?

A. $480
B. $640
C. $590
D. $30

22. To solve $2(5 + 3)^2 - 10$, the first step would be to

A. Multiply 2 by 5
B. Square the 3
C. Add 5 and 3
D. Subtract 10

23. The set {1, 4, 16, 64) is what type of sequence?

A. Arithmetic
B. Geometric
C. Triangular
D. Fibonacci

24. The additive inverse of 4 is

A. 1/4
B. 1
C. 4
D. -4

25. Which of these is NOT an equivalent ratio to the other three?

A. one to three
B. 1:3
C. 2/6
D. 3/1

26. For lunch on Wednesday, students have a choice of pizza or a peanut butter and jelly sandwich. For a drink, they can choose milk, chocolate milk, orange juice, or apple juice. How many combinations of main dishes and drinks are possible?

A. 6
B. 4
C. 8
D. 12

27. The school store sells notebooks and pencils. The ratio of sales today was 2 notebooks to 3 pencils. If the store sold 6 notebooks today, how many pencils did they sell?

A. 3
B. 9
C. 6
D. 12

28. What is the absolute value of -10?

A. 10
B. -10
C. 1/10
D. 1

29. The Pythagorean Theorem is used to find

A. the slope of a line
B. the volume of a cylinder
C. the sides of a right triangle
D. the midpoint of a line segment

30. Put-together problems may contain an unknown

A. product
B. dividend
C. addend
D. divisor

31. The multiples of 6 include

A. 1, 2, and 3
B. 3, 6, and 9
C. 6, 12, and 18
D. .6, 6, and 66

32. Two lines that never intersect are

A. perpendicular
B. complementary
C. parallel
D. supplementary

Question 33 refers to the following diagram:

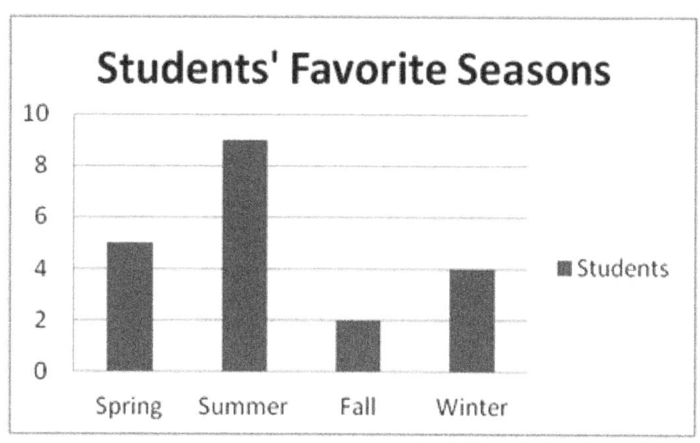

33. **How many more students like summer than fall?**

A. 7.0
B. 11.0
C. 8.0
D. 3.0

34. $a^2 \bullet a^3 =$

A. a^6
B. a^5
C. a^{-1}
D. $a^{2/3}$

35. Which of these numbers is NOT equivalent to the others?

A. 1/2
B. 0.5
C. 2/6
D. 0.50

36. 2 is the only even number that is also

A. rational
B. prime
C. natural
D. irrational

37. Mrs. Nelson's class is 72% male. If there are 25 students in the class, how many students are females?

A. 18
B. 10
C. 7
D. 17

38. Which of these numbers is the smallest in value?

A. .39
B. .317
C. .3564
D. .4

39. On a recent test, five friends had scores of 88, 92, 76, 94, and 80. What was the mean of their scores?

A. 84
B. 86
C. 88
D. 18

40. $3 + 4(1+3)^2 =$

A. 67.0
B. 112.0
C. 100.0
D. 13.0

41. Line A contains the points (2, 4) and (4, 6). What is the slope of the line?

A. 1
B. 2
C. -1
D. 1/2

42. 1, 4, 9, 16, 25... What is the next number in this sequence?

A. 29
B. 39
C. 36
D. 44

43. The measure of the angle that is supplementary to a 70° angle is

A. 110°
B. 20°
C. -70°
D. 30°

44. Which of theses in NOT equal to the other three?

A. .25
B. 25%
C. 25
D. 1/4

45. The greatest common factor (GCF) of 15 and 18 is

A. 3
B. 90
C. 5
D. 18

DIRECTIONS FOR THE OPEN-RESPONSE ITEM ASSIGNMENT

This section of the test consists of an open-response item assignment that appears on the following page. You will be asked to prepare a written response of approximately 150–300 words, or 1–2 pages, for the assignment. You should use your time to plan, write, review, and edit your response for the assignment.

Read the topic and directions for the assignment carefully before you begin to work. Think about how you will organize your response.

As a whole, your response to the assignment must demonstrate an understanding of the knowledge of the field. In your response to the assignment, you are expected to demonstrate the depth of your understanding of the subject area by applying your knowledge rather than by merely reciting factual information.

Your response to the assignment will be evaluated based on the following criteria.

- PURPOSE: the extent to which the response achieves the purpose of the assignment
- SUBJECT KNOWLEDGE: appropriateness and accuracy in the application of subject knowledge
- SUPPORT: quality and relevance of supporting evidence
- RATIONALE: soundness of argument and degree of understanding of the subject area

The open-response item assignment is intended to assess subject knowledge. Your response must be communicated clearly enough to permit valid judgment of the evaluation criteria by scorers. Your response should be written for an audience of educators in this field. The final version of your response should conform to the conventions of edited American English. Your response should be your original work, written in your own words, and not copied or paraphrased from some other work.

Be sure to write about the assigned topic. Please write legibly. You may not use any reference materials during the test. Remember to review your work and make any changes you think will improve your response.

Write or print your response in the space provided following the assignment.

OPEN RESPONSE ITEM ASSIGNMENT

Use the information below to complete the exercise that follows.

Students are asked to solve the following problem:

In the figure above, what is the probability that a randomly selected point within the figure will be located in the shaded region?

Student Response:

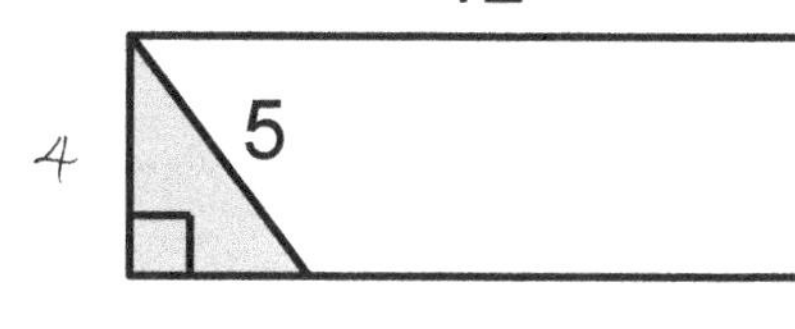

3

Area of Rectangle: $12 \times 4 = 48$

Area of triangle: $4 \times 3 = 12$

Probability $= \frac{12}{48} = \frac{1}{4}$

Use your knowledge of mathematics to create a response in which you:

- correct and explain any errors in the student's work (be sure to provide a correct solution, show your work, and explain your reasoning)
- solve the problem using an alternative method that could enhance the student's conceptual understanding of geometry and probability in the context of the problem

Answers and Explanations

Multi-Subject Subtest

1. B

Igneous rock is formed when magma cools and hardens.

2. B

The nucleus of an atom contains protons, which have a positive charge, and neutrons, which have a neutral charge, making the overall charge of the nucleus positive.

3. B

Hyperbole is the use of exaggeration to make a point. The speaker has not literally been in line forever. The exaggeration is meant to convey that the speaker has been in the line for a very long time.

4. D

The last quatrain tells why the narrator moves on. He has made promises to someone that require him to continue to travel many more miles.

5. D

Latin America is a region, sharing common geographic and cultural characteristics.

6. D

The flower is the site of reproduction in plants.

7. B

Interrogative sentences ask a question and end with a question mark.

8. A

A sentence must contain a noun and a verb.

9. A

Manifest Destiny was the belief that the United States should extend from the Atlantic to the Pacific. These territorial acquisitions helped the nation to reach that goal.

10. C

The circulatory system transports blood throughout the human body through veins and arteries.

11. D

A compound is the result of chemical bonding of two or more elements.

12. C

Tentativeness is the idea that something has been made or done on a trial basis or as an experiment, or is not final or conclusive. As new evidence comes to light, scientific knowledge is revised.

13. A

Natural selection is the process by which those traits that are beneficial to organisms are produced and passed on in the species. Natural selection is based on a premise of the "survival of the fittest," which says that those organisms best genetically equipped to survive and reproduce will and will have their traits passed on. Those organisms that are weaker will eventually die off and with them, their less favorable traits.

14. B

In surface run-off, water remains in liquid form. Run-off occurs when the soil becomes oversaturated with water and the excess comes to the surface and flows over land.

15. C

In this scene from a play by William Shakespeare, one character is speaking directly to another. This is called dialogue.

16. D

A wheel and axle is the most helpful simple machine for moving an object across a horizontal distance. Pulleys and levers are more useful for vertical distances, while wedges are used for cutting or splitting.

17. C

The voting age was lowered to 18 (from 21) nationwide by the 26th Amendment in 1971.

18. D

A control group shows what would happen to the plant normally, if the plant food experiment did not take place, so that the plants that are given the food can be measured against something reliable.

19. B

Tense should be consistent when talking about the same time period. "Moved," "lived," and "works" do not all maintain the same tense.

20. B

A simile is a comparison that uses "like" or "as."

21. B

The Chinese implemented a civil service exam to ensure that government employees were qualified.

22. B

Expository writing is meant to be informative.

23. C

The comparison of how little fence Tom has painted compared with the unpainted fence ahead helps to show how large and daunting Tom found this task to be.

24. B

Tom is very discouraged by the prospect of painting the whole fence and is very reluctant to do so.

25. D

All of these are important safety considerations when using Bunsen burners.

26. C

Equilibrium is achieved when the resultant of all forces acting on an object is zero. This means that the object could either be at rest or in unaccelerated motion.

27. A

During the Middle Ages, political power was decentralized under the feudal system. The Roman Catholic Church became very powerful both in the sacred and secular realms, and it provided a sense of unity throughout Western Europe.

28. D

Some organisms use sexual reproduction, while others utilize asexual reproduction.

29. C

Big business was fairly unregulated in the 19th century, which led to much abuse. Regulations to protect consumers were put into place in the 20th century.

30. A

The Declaration of Independence was sent to the British monarch to demonstrate the intent of the American colonies to form an independent nation.

31. B

From the end of World War II until the dissolution of the Soviet Union in 1991, United States foreign policy was primarily driven by its Cold War competition with the Soviet Union.

32. B

Scarcity of resources means that resources are limited. How limited supplies of resources are to be allocated is foundational to economics.

33. C

A persuasive essay is one in which the author tries to convince the reader of a certain point of view. The only one of these sentences that expresses an opinion rather than a fact is C.

34. A

"Meteorite" is the name given to meteoroids once they enter Earth's atmosphere.

35. C

The idea that an object in motion will stay in motion and an object at rest will stay at rest unless acted upon by an outside force is known as inertia. This is part of Newton's First Law of Motion.

36. B

The esophagus transports food from the mouth to the stomach.

37. B

A bureaucracy is the organizational structure of a government containing the employees and mechanisms that carry out the daily functions of the government.

38. C

Free verse poetry contains neither rhyme nor meter.

39. A

Paleontologists study fossils.

40. B

An oxymoron is a phrase that combines two words with opposite meanings.

41. C

A persuasive essay is one in which the author tries to convince the reader of a certain point of view. The only one of these sentences that expresses an opinion rather than a fact is C.

42. C

The Neolithic Revolution ushered in the era of farming, when permanent settlements became a possibility for the first time because farming meant that people no longer had to migrate to find food by hunting and gathering.

43. C

Revising is making changes to content. This step is followed by editing, which is correcting mechanical issues.

44. B

While other animals adapt to their environments, humans have the ability to change their environments. Modern technology increasingly allows this.

45. C

The balance of trade refers to the ratio of exports to imports that a country has over a period of time. A favorable balance of trade is one in which a country exports more than it imports.

46. B

Topographic maps are physical maps that show elevation.

47. C

In a laissez-faire system, the government is completely hands-off and market forces such as supply and demand are allowed to freely control the economy.

48. D

All of these share the common root “script” which means “write.”

49. C

Affixes are prefixes and suffixes added to the beginning or end of base words to change their meaning.

50. A

The sentence is missing articles such as "a" or "the."

51. B

There are many reasons that people undertake scientific inquiry. Two of the major motivations for scientific exploration are a desire to satisfy curiosity about the world and seeking practical applications of science that will benefit humanity.

52. A

Prior to the Civil War, the country became divided over the issue of slavery and the fact that the Southern states felt that the federal government was infringing on states’ rights by placing limits on slavery.

53. C

The tilt of the Earth on its axis determines how direct the solar radiation a location receives will be.

54. C

Aqueducts—structures used to transport water—were an important part of ancient Roman architecture.

55. B

Phoneme substitution is an exercise in which one phoneme of a word is replaced with another phoneme to create a new word.

Open Response Assignment Sample Answer:

The Protestant Reformation was largely a response to abuses in the Catholic Church. Martin Luther, a German monk, is credited with starting the Reformation when he posted his "95 Theses" to the door of Wittenberg Cathedral in 1517. In this document, Luther called for reforms within the Catholic Church, especially with regard to the corrupt sale of indulgences. The Catholic Church had been selling indulgences, telling people that they could pay money to lessen their own or a loved one's time in purgatory and ensure their salvation. The Church was getting very rich off of this and other corrupt practices. Luther also had doctrinal issues with the Church, arguing that salvation comes through grace alone and not by works. When the Catholic Church refused to make reforms and instead excommunicated Luther, he and his followers started their own church, which became known as the Lutheran Church.

Other reformers, all with varying beliefs, began to follow in Luther's footsteps, spreading their ideas and starting new Christian denominations. The spread of these ideas was aided a newly developed piece of technology—the printing press. The printing press allowed for quick, cheap mass production of Reformation literature and new Bibles printed in the vernacular, helping them spread quickly across the continent. Without the printing press, the Reformation probably could not have had so quick and dramatic an impact on European society.

As a result of the Reformation, many new denominations were formed. This caused the religious, political, social, and economic power of the Catholic Church to decline. It also resulted in conflict between Protestants and Catholics which, in some areas, led to war.

Mathematics Subtest

1. D

The even numbers in this set are 2, 4, and 6. That means that there are 3 favorable outcomes out of 6 possible outcomes. The probability of getting an even number is 3/6, which reduces to 1/2.

2. B

7/8 = 0.875

3. C

Grams are used to measure mass.

4. B

21/25 * 100 = 84

5. A

To convert a mixed number to an improper fraction, multiply the denominator by the whole number and add the numerator.

6. C

Any number raised to the 0 power equals 1.

7. C

98 has factors other than itself and 1, so it is not prime.

8. B

Subtraction can be modeled as a "take-apart" problem, with either an unknown minuend, an unknown subtrahend, or an unknown difference.

9. A

The commutative property states that in a multiplication or addition problem, the order of the numbers being added or multiplied does not affect the final result.

10. B

80 cm = 0.0008 km

11. B

Integers are numbers that do not contain fractional parts (whole numbers and their negatives).

12. A

Remember to switch the inequality sign when dividing each side by a negative number.

13. B

Angles that measure between 90° and 180° are considered obtuse.

14. D

Convert 2 hours and 30 minutes to 2.5 hours. 55 miles per hour multiplied by 2.5 hours equals 137.5 miles.

15. D

You need a common denominator in order to add fractions. Multiplication and division do not require a common denominator, and if the fractions have the same numerator, they can be compared without a common denominator.

16. A

Tiling- splitting a shape into unit squares- can be used to find the area of a rectangle with whole-number side lengths. None of the other shapes listed could be split evenly into unit squares.

17. B

The two numbers are 6 and 2. 6 * 2 = 12 and 6 - 2 = 4.

18. A

Absolute deviation is the distance of a number in a set from the mean. 21.8 - 15.6 = 6.2

19. B

To find the median, put the scores in numerical order. The median is the number is the middle. In order, the numbers read: 76, 80, 88, 92, 94. The number in the middle is 88.

20. A

The formula for the area of a triangle is A =1/2 bh. In this case, the triangle is right so the two shorter sides will represent the base and the height. (The longest side in a right triangle is always the hypotenuse.) 1/2 * 3 * 4 = 6

21. A

If 25 shirts cost $50 from the manufacturer, the cost per shirt is $2. For 80 shirts, the cost would be $160. The sale price per shirt is $8, which comes to $640 for 80 shirts. Profit = price - cost. $640 - $160 = $480

22. C

The first step in the order of operations is to take care of operations within parentheses.

23. B

To get from one member of the set to the next, multiply by 4. A set whose rule is solely multiplication is called a geometric set.

24. D

The additive inverse of a number is its equal opposite such that the two numbers added together would equal zero. 4 + (-4) = 0

25. D

3/1 represents a ratio of 3 to 1, not 1 to 3. 2/6 is a fraction equivalent to 1/3, so it also is an equivalent ratio.

26. A

You can solve this problem by drawing a tree diagram of the possibilities, by listing out the possible combinations, or by using multiplication. 2 choices for sandwiches multiplied by 3 choices for drinks equals 6 possible combinations.

27. B

Solve by setting up a proportion.

28. A

Absolute value is a number’s distance from zero and is always a positive number.

29. C

The Pythagorean Theorem is $a^2+ b\ ^2= c^2$, where a and b are the lengths of the legs of a right triangle and c is the length of the hypotenuse.

30. C

Addition can be modeled as a "put-together" problem, with either an unknown addend or an unknown sum.

31. C

Multiples are the result of multiplying a number by positive integers. 6 * 1 = 6; 6 * 2 = 12; 6 * 3 = 18; etc.

32. C

Lines that never touch are parallel. Perpendicular lines intersect at a right angle. The terms complimentary and supplementary refer to angles, not lines.

33. A

9 students like summer the best and 2 students like fall the best. 9 – 2 = 7

34. B

The product rule of exponents states: $a^n \bullet a^m = a^{n+m}$

35. C

2/6 is equal to 1/3. All of the other choices are equal to 1/2.

36. B

A prime number can only be divided evenly by itself and 1. 2 is the only even number that is prime because every other even number can be divided by 2.

37. C

72% of 25 is 18 (25 * 0.75 = 18). That means there are 18 males in the class. To find out how many females there are, subtract the number of males from the total.

38. B

When comparing decimals, move from left to right. A, B, and C all have a 3 in the tenths place. In the hundredths place, choice B has a 1, which is the smallest of the given values.

39. B

To find the mean, add up the scores and divide by the number of scores (5).

40. A

It is important to follow the order of operations (PEMDAS).

41. A

The slope formula is m = (y_2-y_1)/(x_2-x_1)

42. C

This is a set of perfect squares.

43. A

Supplementary angles add up to 180°.

44. C

.25, 25%, and 1/4 are all equivalent.

45. A

The factors of 15 are 1, 3, 5, and 15. The factors of 18 are 1, 2, 3, 6, 9, and 18. The greatest common factor is 3.

Open Response Assignment Sample Answer

The student correctly found the lengths of the legs of the right triangle, which is one containing the standard 3-4-5 ratio. From there, the student applied the 4 found in the first step to correctly find the area of the rectangle: 12 x 4 = 48.

The student has made an error in finding the area of the triangle. The formula for the area of a triangle is A = ½ bh. The student left out the "½." The area of the triangle should be ½ x 3 x 4 = 6.

The probability that a random point will fall within the shaded region can be expressed as a fraction with the area of the shaded region on top and the total area of the figure on the bottom. This would make the probability $\frac{6}{48}$ *or* $\frac{1}{8}$.

One alternative solution is to approach the problem visually. The rectangle can be evenly divided into triangles of this size. When the triangles are all drawn in, as shown below, there are 8 triangles that fill the rectangle.

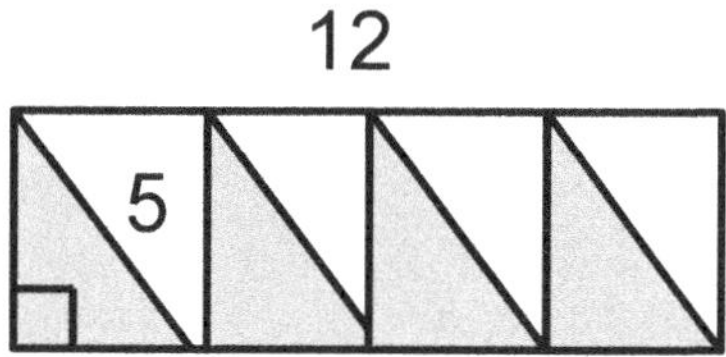

One of these triangles (the original shaded area) takes up $\frac{1}{8}$ *of the total area. The probability of a random point falling within the original shaded area is therefore* $\frac{1}{8}$.

Made in the USA
Middletown, DE
28 July 2019